Publishing on the eve of the soccer World Cup in the United States, Mexico, and Canada, this concise, power-packed philippic provides a critical take on the dark underbelly of the beautiful game at its most storied moment.

At the heart of this analysis by acclaimed sportswriter and scholar Jules Boykoff, who himself played soccer professionally, is the concept of sportswashing, where political leaders use sports to stoke nationalism and legitimize themselves on the world stage, deflecting from chronic problems at home. Step forward the recipient of the newly cast FIFA Peace Prize, Donald J. Trump, a titan unrivaled in squeegeeing every drop of personal wealth and prestige from hosting the competition. In this, he is ably assisted by a governing body of global soccer dripping in patronage and corruption.

In these pages Boykoff demonstrates that it is possible to simultaneously treasure the skills and athleticism displayed on the pitch while lamenting their exploitation by malevolent powerbrokers for whom love of the game means nothing next to turning a buck or harvesting prestige. And, as *Red Card* so skillfully shows, this bait and switch is not confined to soccer. Precisely the same legerdemain will be used to distract and enrich when the Olympic Games come to Los Angeles two years from now.

"We urgently need writers and thinkers like Boykoff to encourage us to reclaim the people's game for the communities it is supposed to serve." —**NICK MCGEEHAN**

"Essential reading for anyone who truly loves the beautiful game and believes in sport's real values of integrity, inclusion, and human rights." —**ANDREA FLORENCE**

"Jules Boykoff's new book is indispensable reading for those who want to make sense of the gradual degeneration of international football and how to reclaim the beauty within the game." —**KARIM ZIDAN**

"There is no one better equipped than Boykoff to interrogate the FIFA World Cup . . . he critiques it with nuance, intelligence, and vigour . . . a must-read for anyone interested in football, transparency, and truth." —**SHIREEN AHMED**

"It is as erudite as it is earnest. Boykoff's searing criticism doesn't leave you feeling defeated, but rather, hopeful that we can breathe life back into football." —**BRENDA ELSEY**

RED CARD

RED CARD

The 2026 World Cup, Sportswashing, and the FIFA Greed Machine

JULES BOYKOFF

Introduction by DAVE ZIRIN

O/R

OR Books

New York • London • Kolkata

Published by OR Books, New York and London

Visit our website at www.orbooks.com

First printing 2026

The manufacturer's authorised representative in the EU for product safety is Authorised Rep Compliance Ltd, 71 Lower Baggot Street, Dublin D02 P593 Ireland (www.arccompliance.com)

Typeset by Lapiz Digital. Printed by BookMobile, USA, and CPI, UK.

OR Books
40 Loisaida Avenue
NY, NY 10009

paperback ISBN 978-1-68219-528-4• ebook ISBN 978-1-68219-529-1

For Kaia Sand and Jessi Wahnetah

Epigraphs

"No Normal Sport in an Abnormal Society."
— South African Council on Sport anti-apartheid slogan

"The very quality of propaganda—illogic—is precisely its strongest suit, because it is a distraction."
— Mohammed El-Kurd, *Perfect Victims and the Politics of Appeal*

"Politics does not reflect majorities, it constructs them."
— Stuart Hall, *The Hard Road to Renewal: Thatcherism and the Crisis of the Left*

"Memory a wind passing through the blood trees within us."
— Carolyn Forché, *The Angel of History*

Contents

Introduction by Dave Zirin 1

Chapter 1: Here Comes the Sportswash 9

Chapter 2: Trump, Sports, and Sportswashing 21

Chapter 3: The FIFA Beast, Authoritarianism, and the World Cup 37

Chapter 4: Sportswashing and the World Cup in Russia and Qatar 61

Chapter 5: The 2026 World Cup from Bid to Delivery: Controversies Arise 81

Chapter 6: The World Cup, Sportswashing, and Activist Fightback 107

Conclusion: A Blast from the Future 129

Notes 139

Acknowledgments 169

Introduction to *Red Card*

DAVE ZIRIN

"The word 'FIFA' is about as popular here as 'FEMA' in New Orleans after Katrina."

— *Dylan Stillwood, journalist in Brazil, 2014.*

I never thought I'd see Brazilians protest soccer. As a New Yorker, the equivalent would be—so I thought at the time—a mass movement against sausage with extra cheese. But there I was in Rio de Janeiro at a mass march against Brazil's 2014 staging of the World Cup. What I witnessed would change the course of Brazilian history, and not in a direction anyone who believes in human rights or the rule of law would want to travel.

Brazil's left-wing firebrand president, Luiz Inácio "Lula" Da Silva, had successfully bid on the Cup in 2007 and promised that the event would be a staggering success: economically, politically, and culturally. The world would come to Brazil, spend their money, and rejoice in the glory of the beautiful game in the country that had done more to make the game "beautiful" than any nation on earth. And yet in the summer of 2013, one million people took to the streets, the largest protests since the fall of the country's dictatorship three decades earlier, with untold thousands marching toward the stadiums hosting the World Cup's precursor, the Confederations Cup.

While 2007 was a period of what appeared to be endless growth for Brazil, 2013 had ushered in a time of austerity and privation that made the World Cup look like a sinful waste of resources. These protesters held a number of issues close to their hearts: they were against the cutbacks being inflicted on Lula's popular social programs, against a historically unparalleled rise in bus fares, and against the Copa coming to Brazil. In truth, it was not so much that they were protesting soccer or even the World Cup. They were taking to the streets against all the detritus the event leaves in its wake: namely, spiraling debt, the militarization of public space, and the building or refurbishing of new soccer facilities across the country to meet the needs of FIFA, not the local football clubs that played there. These billion-dollar "white elephants," as they were called, were decried because of the profligate waste they openly represented.

If there is one resource this country of 200 million people, with a landmass larger than the continental United States, does not lack, it is soccer stadiums.

The new "white elephants" were built in areas with beautiful surroundings—even in the Amazon rainforest—but these were also places without soccer teams or even without a local interest in soccer. (Yes, those areas do exist in Brazil.)

People began to view these structures like poisonous weeds, at odds not only with the people's needs but also with the environmental protections promised by the Workers' Party government. The Amazon is known as "the lungs of the earth," and a soccer stadium being dropped in its midst is hardly a breathing aid. The demonstrations against these stadiums were met with violence to silence dissent; the left-wing government sent in troops to shoot tear gas and concussion grenades into the crowds. Laws were passed criminalizing protest, and yet slogans such as #NãoVaiTerCopa (There Will Be No Cup) still dotted the landscape.

"FIFA is the real president of our country," said legendary Brazilian soccer star Romário at the time. "FIFA comes to our country and imposes a state within a state. It's not going to pay taxes, it's going to come, install a circus without paying anything and take everything with it. They are taking the piss out of us with our money, the public's money. The money that has been spent on Mané Garrincha stadium could have been used to build 150,000 housing units."

And yet, Lula was undeterred. In 2014, he said, "This Cup will serve as a lesson to the pessimist." Although Lula had stepped down in 2011, this perspective—not listening to the protesters and instead hoping for consent at the end of a truncheon—continued under the new Workers' Party leader, Dilma Rousseff, who had assumed the presidency. When I was in Brazil for the 2014 World Cup, the protests continued. People chanted against the Cup, calling for an end to the rampant corruption surrounding stadium construction contracts—news of which was leaking by the day—and a rethinking of the nation's priorities. These demonstrations were put down ruthlessly. As a journalist, getting doused with military-grade gas until I needed to pour milk into my eyes to quell the sting, or the way my ears rang to the point of abject confusion with every concussion grenade, were physical—not to mention mental—sensations that I won't soon forget.

Imagine the political confusion that ensued: One million people in the streets asking for state relief to a crisis built upon austerity, inflicted by leaders who had installed a social democracy that had previously aided workers and the poor in unprecedented ways. Leaders who had devoted their lives to fighting a dictatorship, prioritizing the World Cup over workers' lives, and quashing their dissent. It led to mass confusion, demoralization, and, I would argue, opened the door to someone who was barely a blip on the political screen when I was in Brazil: a far-right politician with a taste for violence named Jair Bolsonaro, who won the presidency in 2019.

Bolsonaro quickly revealed himself to be a charmless, anti-democratic goon. The people's disgust with Bolsonarism—basically an uglier version of Trumpism without the Atlantic City smarm—was immediate. His administration immediately gorged itself on opportunities for corruption and relished in banning books, sending in police and the military to break up political meetings, and throttling freedoms untouched since the fall of the dictatorship. Bolsonaro was unceremoniously booted from office after one term in 2023. He then—with encouragement from US Trumpists—attempted his own version of the January 6, 2021, ransacking of the US Capitol in hopes of overturning the election. Even worse than Trump, his aim was a full-scale military coup. Bolsonaro failed in these efforts and—unlike the way we do things in the United States—was actually prosecuted for his crimes and sentenced to twenty-seven years in prison. The lesson is that the staging of the World Cup can benefit the right-wing politicians and military juntas waiting in the wings.

The warnings of 2014 were not heeded in Brazil. In 2026, even more danger signs loom in the United States. Donald Trump is attempting to use what's being called "the joyless World Cup" for reasons that have nothing to do with soccer and everything to do with advancing an authoritarian agenda.

In *Red Card,* Jules Boykoff breaks it down piece by piece: how Trump is trying to exploit this World Cup, why we must resist, and the ways that Trump's actions are lubricated by FIFA's own history of cozying up to dictatorships and aiding countries with human-rights records that would make a 1930s fascist blush. While FIFA has been managed as an engine of right-wing corruption and greed for decades, the current chief, Gianni "Johnny Boy" Infantino, might be the worst of them all. We need to understand every political dynamic of the World Cup, or our own country will further travel down this bottomless rabbit hole of Trumpist right-wing degradation.

Thank the heavens we have Jules Boykoff to make all of this plain and clear for ourselves and the soccer fans in our lives. Boykoff is perhaps the finest theorist of sports mega-events like the World Cup and the Olympics in the

English-speaking world. His razor-sharp insight arrives through his status as an insider to the sport: a former US under-23 national team player and professional footballer, someone who loves the Beautiful Game but cannot stand how it's been exploited for ends that have nothing to do with adjectives pertaining to beauty.

Boykoff has penned a wild historical ride, bracing in its verisimilitude and with an analysis as powerful as a Roberto Carlos corner kick. This book is for leftists who love soccer—and may even plan on watching the 2026 World Cup—who want to understand how authoritarians like Trump use the people's game to engage in sportswashing. Lace up your cleats. It's time for *Red Card*.

1

Here Comes the Sportswash

Soccer is never just soccer. And sports are politics by other means.

This was abundantly clear when the powerbrokers of world football convened in December 2025 for the 2026 FIFA World Cup draw. Glitz and glam were in abundance. Supermodel Heidi Klum emceed the event alongside actor Kevin Hart. The audience included a Who's Who of North American sports icons: NBA great Shaquille O'Neal, hockey Hall of Famer Wayne Gretzky, NFL Super Bowl champions Tom Brady, and New England Patriots owner—and Epstein files staple—Robert Kraft. The event featured the heads of state from all three host countries: Canadian Prime Minister Mark Carney, Mexican President Claudia Sheinbaum, and US President Donald Trump. To close the show, the Village People played its MAGA anthem "YMCA," a brazen sop to Trump. The point of the event—sorting the 48 countries into twelve groups to compete in the World Cup—was relegated to a mere sideshow, lost amid the star-studded bromide-o-rama.

The event took place in Washington, DC, at the John F. Kennedy Center for the Performing Arts, renamed later that month "The Donald J. Trump and The John F. Kennedy Memorial Center for the Performing Arts" before being shut down when numerous artists refused to perform there. FIFA relocated the event from Las Vegas to make it as convenient as possible for Trump to attend. The switch was orchestrated by FIFA President Gianni Infantino, a man who had long made a tactical habit of sucking up to the powerful.

Infantino took his sycophancy to the next level at the 2026 World Cup draw, awarding Trump with the inaugural FIFA Peace Prize, a wholly confected accolade with no precedent, let alone serious criteria. The award—technically titled "FIFA Peace Prize – Football Unites the World"—was concocted the previous month "to reward individuals who have taken exceptional and extraordinary actions for peace and by doing so have united people across the world."[1] Infantino's unilateral decision to establish the award blindsided his colleagues at the FIFA Council, composed of eight vice-presidents, 28 members at large, and chaired by Infantino himself. Some FIFA Council members first heard about the prize by reading a press release. When Human Rights Watch wrote to FIFA to request basic information about the prize—its search criteria, the nomination process, the judges for the award—the group was unceremoniously stonewalled.

The design of the trophy itself was downright bizarre: a gaudy assemblage of thin, grizzled hands that looked as if they were surfacing from the bowels of hell, stretching toward a golden orb hovering above. Infantino, who vocally supported Trump's failed bid to win the Nobel Peace Prize, which instead went to Venezuela's right-wing opposition leader María Corina Machado, took to the stage to explain why he chose Trump for the award: "This is what we want from a leader, a leader that cares about the people. We want to live in a safe world, in a safe environment. We want to unite. That's what we do here today. That's what we do at the World Cup, Mr. President, and you definitely deserve the first FIFA Peace Prize for your action, for what you have obtained in *your* way, but you obtained it in an incredible way." Infantino went on to gush, "You can always count, Mr. President, on my support, on the support of the entire football community, or soccer community, to help you make peace and make the world prosper all over the world."[2]

Because Trump is a megalomaniac with a crude, transactional governing style and zero commitment to truth, he is well situated to leverage the toxic gangsterism of sports. “The truth is that sport, in its current hyper-politicized and hyper-commodified form, is exquisitely suited to Trump’s needs,” wrote Bryan Armen Graham in the *Guardian*. “It supplies the crowds, the cameras, the ritual patriotism and the ready-made mythologies of strength and struggle. It gives him stadiums and arenas that can be turned into instant rallies and backstage corridors that double as donor gatherings.” In addition, Graham notes, “It offers him a role he prefers to the one described in the constitution: not head of the executive branch, but ringmaster-in-chief.”[3]

Infantino has been Trump’s primary enabler when it comes to converting soccer into political advantage. He has visited the White House and Mar-a-Lago more than any world leader, so many times that Trump might start charging him rent. In fact, after Infantino established a New York headquarters in Trump Towers, he actually *is* paying rent to Trump.[4] Gianni Infantino is Trump’s principal accomplice when it comes to sportswashing.

Sportswashing is when political leaders use sports to appear important or legitimate on the world stage while stoking nationalism and deflecting attention from chronic social problems and human-rights woes at home. Sportswashers use sports to try to burnish national prestige, to convey economic or political success, to spur personal enrichment. Sportswashing fortifies the bones of global capitalism while reconfiguring the meaning of fandom, allegiance, and human rights. It targets both domestic and international audiences. It has significant material implications, facilitating what economic geographer David Harvey calls a "spatial fix"—moving surplus capital elsewhere and making it productive while diversifying a country's investment portfolio. Beyond the money shuffle, sportswashing also plays a vital role in global discourse, subtly massaging reputational repair into public consciousness through the passion and popularity of sport. Importantly, sportswashing can also pave a path for war.[5]

The global sports industry is big money, no question about it. It rakes in at least $2.655 trillion annually, placing it among the top ten revenue-producing industries globally; the United States makes up 40 percent of that total.[6] Sports ownership and rights-holding go hand in hand with astronomical plutocracy. The largest private landowner in the United States is Stan Kroenke, the billionaire whose holding company owns Arsenal in the Premier League, Arsenal Women of the Women's Super League, the Colorado Rapids of Major League Soccer, the NFL's Los Angeles Rams, the NBA's Denver Nuggets, the NHL's Colorado Avalanche, and other sports teams.[7]

And sports are enormously popular. One estimate found that 95 percent of the global population recognized the Olympic rings. The FIFA World Cup is the most-watched sports event on Earth. An estimated 1.5 billion people tuned in for the 2022 World Cup final between Argentina and France, while some 5 billion tuned in at some point during the tournament.[8] The 2026 World Cup, with the field increased to 48 teams, promises to shatter these records.

In Chapter 2, I will map Trump's relationship to sports and explain how the World Cup presents him with a once-in-a-generation chance to flex raw power over the most popular sport in the world, gifting the grifter-in-chief with an extraordinary sportswashing opportunity. Although sportswashing could only fully emerge in an era of hyper-mobile capital and a celebrity-drenched sports culture with trillions flowing through it, key building blocks of sportswashing surfaced over time. In Chapter 3, I offer important examples from history, such as Benito Mussolini's use of the 1934 World Cup and the 1978 tournament overseen by an Argentinian military junta, with assistance from Henry Kissinger. In Chapter 4, I examine two instructive cases of full-fledged sportswashing in the twenty-first century: the 2018 World Cup in Russia and the 2022 tournament in Qatar. In Chapters 5 and 6, I lay out how sportswashing has unfolded—and continues to unfold—in the United States, where Trump is aggressively using sports to appear important on the world stage while stoking nationalism, and bolstering the militarized state security apparatus. As we shall see, the 2026 World Cup is quickening the slide toward autocracy, helping Trump—and the United States more generally—become ever more authoritarian. In those chapters I also catalog activists' fightback against sportswashing and a burgeoning movement to boycott the tournament. I conclude the book by arrowing forward in time toward sports mega-events like the Los Angeles 2028 Summer Olympics, which are slated to be held under President Trump, and the 2034 Saudi Arabia World Cup. Both events will take place under the spell of sportswashing. This is an idea that's not going away anytime soon.

I care deeply about the sport of soccer. I spent a lot of time playing the game: as a scholarship athlete at the University of Portland, as a member of the US under-23 men's national soccer team, as a professional for four years with three teams. I believe deeply in the power of sport to connect, to enrich, to sinter. The people entrusted to cultivate global football have enormous power, and with that power comes responsibility. Unfortunately, the barons at FIFA have failed in their responsibility to govern the game with equity or ethics. Sportswashing allows these cartoon villains to take their exploitation to a whole new level.

When I played professional soccer in the mid-1990s I would often decompress after a match by listening to Dmitri Shostakovich's string quartets on my Sony Discman D-45 portable CD player. Little did I know that Shostakovich was a lifelong football aficionado, a hardcore supporter of FC Zenit, later renamed Zenit St. Petersburg. He even composed a ballet in 1930, "The Golden Age," depicting a Soviet soccer team competing against a squad from the bourgeois decadent West, replete with a section titled "Football" that commenced with a referee's whistle. Shostakovich made arrangements to attend the 1966 World Cup in England—where the Soviet Union placed fourth—but he suffered a heart attack in May of that year and wasn't able to attend. Instead, he watched from a hospital bed.[9]

Shostakovich described football as "the ballet of the masses." For him, the sport refracted politics, culture, class struggle. It was a zone of art, a theater of invention, a space of yearning and desire. Or, as Umberto Eco put it, "Sport is Society."[10] Many a leftist has contemplated soccer's political possibilities. Antonio Gramsci once dubbed soccer "an open-air kingdom of human loyalty."[11] Frantz Fanon embedded football in his therapy regimen for patients, as he believed it played a vital role in their re-socialization.[12] Soccer can crack open space where the normal codes don't apply, where men can embrace other men and perhaps even kiss them and no one blinks, where kids have community etched into the chalk and bone of their malleable minds. In that liminal space, politics can vibrate at an ineffable yet discernible frequency, one that brims with possibility.

Outside of the World Cup draw in DC, activists gathered amid a snowstorm to protest Trumpian sportswashing, to connect the political dots. They brandished signs reading, "No Cup with ICE" and "Red card for war crimes." They chanted, "Soccer is the world's game. ICE is the world's shame."[13] Football, they showed, can be a focal point for fightback.

And yet, modern-day football is also a juggernaut of inequality, a vector of profit for FIFA and its collaborators. Soccer, with its millionaire players, billionaire club owners, and multi-billion-dollar cipher—FIFA—has become bubble-wrapped in analytics that conservatize the game, rendering anachronistic the likes of footballing greats such as Diego Maradona or Marta, geniuses of the game who refused to conform to the dictates of ruthless efficiency. But to cede the topography of football to reactionary forces is to sacrifice an ideological battleground against fascism. Nowhere is this clearer than in the United States, where Donald Trump is leveraging the power of sport to his political advantage with more fervor than any president in US history.

And while "the machinery of spectacle grinds up everything in its path," as Uruguayan writer Eduardo Galeano noted, the glittering social beauty of soccer somehow survives.[14] This is something worth fighting for.

2

Trump, Sports, and Sportswashing

Amid the hubbub of the 2025 presidential inauguration, FIFA boss Gianni Infantino's unmistakable pate could be spotted bobbing in the back row of the VIP section, only meters from where President Trump took the oath of office. Camera in hand, Infantino recorded the proceedings for future use on Instagram, where he documents his every cringy kowtow as Trump's smarmy sidekick. Infantino was situated only a few rows behind former US presidents Joe Biden, Barack Obama, George W. Bush, and Bill Clinton. His proximity to power was absurd but instructive.

Donald Trump's 2025 inauguration foreshadowed the rejiggering of the political power map in Washington, DC. The ceremony featured a gaggle of sycophantic tech billionaires—the likes of Elon Musk, Jeff Bezos, Mark Zuckerberg, Tim Cook of Apple, and Google's Sundar Pichai—some standing right behind the Trump family while AI huckster Sam Altman milled about. The inaugural festivities also included numerous sports personalities. Influencer-boxer Jake Paul and his brother, the wrestler-influencer Logan Paul, attended, at one point snapping a selfie with Irish MMA fighter Conor McGregor, notorious for losing a civil case for rape. UFC CEO Dana White—who has been chummy with Trump for decades—was there alongside prominent podcaster and UFC color commentator Joe Rogan. Boxer Mike Tyson and other sports stars of yore also made the inauguration guest list.[15]

But Infantino's presence marked a significant moment for the FIFA boss, an ascension to the rarefied heights of US political power. A year later he would attend the inaugural meeting of Trump's so-called Board of Peace, where he donned a MAGA-style USA baseball cap, pumped a fist, and gave a thumbs up. This, despite a provision in the FIFA Statutes reading, "FIFA remains neutral in matters of politics and religion." The perennially corrupt International Olympic Committee, where Infantino is a member, swiftly cleared him of violating its neutrality rules.[16] FIFA didn't even bother to consider the matter.

Infantino had already established his unabashed brand of supplication to the world's oligarchs, but with Trump, he was taking his obsequiousness to a new level. Infantino is the pulsing id of the FIFA greed machine, an acquiescent jester willing to shape-shift for the sake of accumulating power. But this jester is walking off with a sack of cash: FIFA expects more than $11 billion in revenues from the 2026 World Cup, a staggering sum that surpasses the gross domestic product of more than sixty countries, including some that will participate in the tournament, such as Cabo Verde and Curaçao.[17]

The 2026 World Cup is sloshing in Infantino and Trump's symbiotic sleaze. Infantino treats the United States like FIFA's private money pump while Trump gets to appear important, lording his mug over the biggest, most-watched sporting event on earth, gleaning football's shine.

Trump has used sports to his political advantage more than any previous US president. Engaging with sports—and sports powerbrokers—was key to his reelection in 2024. Dallas Mavericks owner Miriam Adelson funneled $100 million into Trump's campaign coffers, while both she and Houston Rockets owner Tilman Fertitta each forked over another $1 million to the Trump-Vance Inaugural Committee.

On the campaign trail, Trump went on numerous popular mixed-martial arts podcasts with massive audiences of young men, talking about sports more than politics, and raising the possibility that engaging with the sphere of sports can be *more politically effective* by being *less explicitly political.*

A few months before the election, Trump attended a UFC fight in New Jersey, where fans chanted, "We love Trump!" Former professional wrestler Hulk Hogan spoke at the Republican National Convention. NFL defensive end Nick Bosa seemed to don a MAGA hat at nearly every opportunity, while NFL kicker Harrison Butker started a PAC to support Trump-aligned conservative causes. Just days before the election, Trump sat for a three-hour interview with UFC talking head Joe Rogan. UFC honcho Dana White speechified at Trump's victory celebration. NHL great Wayne Gretzky stood in the wings, sporting a MAGA cap. The list goes on.[18]

After his election, Trump has continued to exploit sports for his right-wing political project. Trump's virulent attack on transgender athletes was not only a go-to move on the campaign stump, but also a crude way to rally his bigoted base once back in office. Once in office, Trump tossed his reactionary supporters red meat through a slew of executive orders related to sport, including "Keeping Men Out of Women's Sports" and "Saving College Sports."[19]

As president, Trump popped up at numerous high-profile sporting events. In November 2025, he became the first US President in over fifty years to attend a regular-season NFL game, even swinging through the FOX broadcast booth for some awkward on-air sports banter.[20] He attended the Daytona 500, the NCAA wrestling championships, the US Open tennis final. And he has actively hyped "UFC Freedom 250," a mixed-martial arts event to be staged on the White House South Lawn in mid-June to celebrate the nation's 250th birthday. The event, scheduled only a few days after the World Cup kicks off, is produced by—you guessed it—the UFC. It just so happens to also land on Trump's eightieth birthday.[21] "Trump isn't athletic," opined a columnist from *The Globe and Mail,* "but he is the [2025] sportsperson of the year. No one has wielded so much influence in the past 12 months."[22]

Trump took his strategic sports scheming to new heights after the US men's hockey team won gold at the Milano Cortina 2026 Olympics. On a locker room phone call with the squad, Trump invited them to the White House and spewed sexist drivel about feeling forced to also invite the gold-medal-winning women's hockey team, lest he be impeached. The players guffawed along, many of them having praised Trump in the past. Then, two days later, the president turned the players into political pawns, rolling them out at his State of the Union Address. "Our country is winning again," he said, "And to prove that point...here with us is a group of winners who just made the entire nation proud. The men's gold medal Olympic hockey team." He even announced that he'd be giving the US goaltender the Presidential Medal of Freedom, the US government's highest civilian honor, joining recent awardees like Charlie Kirk, Rudy Giuliani, and Ben Carson. To be sure, many of the hockey players were perfectly happy to align with the regime. They started chanting "USA! USA!" while pumping their fists and flashing their medals during a nearly two-minute standing ovation, approaching North Korean levels of blunt political puffery and squandering the goodwill they earned after winning gold. "What special champions you are," remarked Trump.[23]

Trump's popularity—what's left of it—is underpinned by a dense network of connections in the sports world. "While Donald Trump has long used sports as a stage to launder his reputation, promote his brand, and propagate his political ideology, his efforts have never been a solo act," writes journalist Karim Zidan. "He has consistently relied on a sprawling cast of athletes, sports executives, media influencers, and politicians to bring his sports spectacles to life and to legitimize his place in the cultural mainstream."[24]

With his loyal jester Gianni Infantino perpetually at the ready, the 2026 World Cup is a prime opportunity for Trump to slide from sports to sportswashing. Trump often talks about how this sports mega-event is among the occasions in his second term that gets his despotic heart beating the quickest. "This is a big deal, I'll tell you," he said at a press event with Infantino in August 2025. "I was so happy to get it—the 2026 FIFA World Cup...It's going to be so exciting for our country."[25]

Trump and Infantino's very public bromance novel has many chapters: at the 2025 FIFA Club World Cup, Infantino gifted Trump with a replica trophy; he allowed Trump to photobomb the tournament's victory celebration with Chelsea FC and even pocket a winner's medal; he attended the Summit for Peace at the behest of Trump in Sharm El-Sheikh, Egypt, in October 2025, where a ceasefire between Israel and Hamas was announced. Infantino dutifully heaps praise on Trump at every opportunity. The ego fluff is a key ingredient for sportswashing. Infantino's toadying—and his emphasis on staging a safe, secure event—enables Trump to turbocharge his violent deportation machine, which is already whirring at a disturbing pitch.

Sportswashing provides Trump with a strategy. In FIFA, he has a more-than-willing partner. FIFA has long preferred dictators to democracies, as we shall see in more detail in Chapters 3 and 4. From the perspective of self-important sports barons, working with autocrats to stage mega-events like the World Cup and the Olympics can bring significant benefits. Former FIFA Secretary General Jérôme Valcke made this clear: "I will say something which is crazy, but less democracy is sometimes better for organizing a World Cup...When you have a very strong head of state who can decide, as maybe Putin can do in 2018...that is easier for us organizers."[26] Substitute Infantino for Valcke and an increasingly authoritarian Trump for Putin, and FIFA's preferred recipe for success remains in place. FIFA's weak claims of political neutrality enable authoritarians to sportswash, offering the imprimatur of cultural legitimacy on scoundrels and human-rights violators.

And let's be absolutely clear: the US is no longer a fully functioning democracy. Under Trump, we're witnessing the slow-motion slide into authoritarianism. Hosting the World Cup unequivocally assists with this grim descent. With the tournament less than six months away, the president—amid the throes of yet another Trumpian charm offensive minus the charm—even stated the quiet part out loud: "Sometimes you need a dictator."[27]

The thing is, he wasn't kidding. The United States is now a place where fair elections that the ruling party does not win are deemed crooked so that ultimately the crooked elections can be deemed fair. The point is not to have people believe all the lies, but to not be able to know what is truth. With Trump in the lead, asset plunder has emerged as a mode of governance. As we shall see, sportswashing facilitates brazen self-enrichment for Trump, his family, and his associates. Meanwhile, he has stripped the varnish from liberal internationalism, and this structures permission for extreme human-rights violations.

This is not merely my own political opinion. Top scholars of democracy argue that, under Trump, the US has fully strayed from the democratic fold. "The United States has descended into competitive authoritarianism," wrote the political scientists Steven Levitsky, Lucan A. Way, and Daniel Ziblatt in early 2026, "a system in which parties compete in elections but incumbents routinely abuse their power to punish critics and tilt the playing field against their opposition."[28] Under competitive authoritarianism, "rules or regulations are enforced selectively, targeting political foes, [and] the law becomes a weapon."[29]

Trump has fully weaponized the criminal legal system while Immigration and Customs Enforcement (ICE) is a barely-regulated paramilitary force invading city after city, factory after factory, neighborhood after neighborhood. Cruelty and caprice—Trumpian signature traits—are two arrows in the autocrat's quiver. (And not exactly behavior that's very becoming of a FIFA Peace Prize recipient!) And the in-your-face symbolism of grandiose self-aggrandizement abounds: not unlike Stalin and Hitler, Trump maniacally renames things after himself, whether buildings (like the Kennedy Center for the Performing Arts, where the World Cup draw was staged), "Trump Accounts" for newborns, or "Trump Gold Cards" for wealthy people seeking legal residence in the US. He even pressured Senate Democrat Chuck Schumer to rename Dulles Airport and Penn Station after him in exchange for a tranche of funding for a rail tunnel under the Hudson River.[30] The Trump regime oscillates from kakistocracy to plutocracy while bald-faced kleptocracy and a wince-worthy cult of personality sit out in the open for all to witness. With competitive authoritarianism, the opposition still maintains channels whereby it can contest authoritarian power, but by the end of 2025, the US stopped being a functioning democracy. And yet, the fight is far from done. The 2026 World Cup, meaning as much as it does to Trump, is therefore a key terrain of political struggle.

If deflecting attention from entrenched domestic social problems and human-rights violations is a key element of sportswashing, what is Trump attempting to deflect our attention from? Well, many things. There are his historically low approval ratings. There's his close relationship with convicted sex offender Jeffrey Epstein. There's the lingering inflation that he promised to fix "on day one." There's the ever-weakening US dollar. There's the $1,000-per-family negative impact that his tariffs are unleashing. There are the weak job numbers. There's the fact that the US is edging toward a recession.

But it's important to note that sportswashing in the United States is a bipartisan affair. Democrats have been more than happy to help. For instance, President Joe Biden gifted Trump with a secret weapon for his sportswashing arsenal: the National Special Security Event designation, or NSSE, created by President Bill Clinton in the late 1990s. In 2024, Biden designated the LA Olympics as an NSSE some four full years ahead of the Games—the furthest in advance of an event *ever.*[31] What does this mean? For starters, it means the NSSE is already in effect and will be in place for the World Cup. Second, when an event such as the World Cup, the Olympics, a Super Bowl, or a military parade is designated as a National Special Security Event by a president or their Department of Homeland Security, it triggers widespread latitude for numerous federal agencies, including ICE. This is a huge deal for numerous World Cup host cities with sizable immigrant populations—places such as Los Angeles, host to eight matches and home to around a million undocumented people. ICE has been running wild in Los Angeles, at times looking like an invasion force. National Special Security Event status only emboldens impunity. The security crackdown on ICE protests in Minneapolis, Chicago, and Los Angeles, sometimes featuring the National Guard and Marines, offers us a frontal view at what mega-event "security" might look like at the 2026 World Cup. Sportswashing is not just about soft power, which the originator of the term, Joseph Nye, asserted, "rests on the ability to shape the preferences of others" through attraction rather than coercion.[32] Sportswashing is about amassing hard power that can be used to suppress dissent.

Sportswashing can slip into two traps. The first is a tendency to only apply it to authoritarian settings. It certainly occurs in autocracies, but can emerge in any political system where leaders use sports mega-events to convey prestige and deflect attention, including the United States. To think otherwise is to willfully apply ideological blinders, to waggle a finger at the Global South while turning a blind eye to the colonizer Global North.

Sportswashing's other trap has to do with audience. When people ask if sportswashing "works," the subtext is typically whether it affects global audiences. And yet, sportswashing is also designed for domestic constituencies. On the home front, sportswashing can galvanize patriotism and national prestige as well as perceptions of political or economic progress. It helps manufacture consent. Sports mega-event organizers capitalize on the opportunity to thicken their ties with other domestic powerbrokers. National and local governments use the events to strategically multiply and militarize their weapons stocks, to create special domestic laws during the sporty state of exception that they'd never be able to get away with during normal political times. So, sportswashing is a social relationship that entangles multiple audiences—both international and domestic—and has long-term effects.

Trump has long viewed sports as an ingredient to his success. "I've always been a football fan. I love sports," he wrote in his 1987 book *The Art of the Deal*. He devoted an entire chapter to his short stint as owner of the New Jersey Generals of the United States Football League, or USFL, writing that "having my own team seemed the realization of a great fantasy." Although journalist Morgan Campbell notes, "Trump drove the fledgling league straight into a ditch,"[33] unsurprisingly, Trump offloaded the blame onto others. "If there was a single key miscalculation I made with the USFL," he wrote, "it was evaluating the strength of my fellow owners. In any partnership, you're only as strong as your weakest link."[34]

But the *other* football—the world's most popular sport—affords a whole new level of opportunity. Of the 2026 World Cup, Trump noted, while Infantino nodded along in agreement, "It's like having many Super Bowls in a short period of time. Because each one of these games, essentially, is a Super Bowl. Some of them are bigger than Super Bowls, actually."[35] Amid the rising tide of authoritarianism globally, and in numerous countries where football is by far the number one sport, Trump will be able to sportswash, looking important on the world's stage while teeing up political and economic wins. As we will see in Chapter 3, Trump is tapping a rich vein of history. Authoritarians latching onto soccer is a wicked tradition of sorts.

3

The FIFA Beast, Authoritarianism, and the World Cup

The origins of the phrase of sportswashing are quite recent. The term was coined in 2015 by human-rights campaigners Gulnara Akhundova and Rebecca Vincent to raise concerns about the European Games in Baku, Azerbaijan.[36] Vincent described sportswashing as an attempt by Azerbaijan's dictator Ilham Aliyev "to distract from its human rights record with prestigious sponsorship and hosting of events." Sportswashing swiftly gained traction in the media sphere. By 2022, Collins Dictionary listed the term among its top ten words of the year.[37] Human-rights groups like Amnesty International and Human Rights Watch folded sportswashing into their portfolios. Academics began to theorize sportswashing, examining its political, cultural, and economic complexity. Political leaders increasingly realized that sportswashing provided a path to diversify their economies, to sop up surplus capital—especially from fossil-fuels—in ways that kept their assets in motion. One could stoke national—and personal—enrichment, and cloak it all in popular sports.

Although sportswashing could only fully emerge in the twentieth century after the comprehensive commercialization of sport—when capital had not only become more globally mobile, but had also flooded the sports world—it's not some blunt rupture in the time-space continuum. Its core features emerged and morphed over time.

Political leaders have long used sports for propagandistic purposes. Recall the "bread and circuses" of ancient Rome. The ancient Olympics in Greece provide another example. In 416 BCE, as war raged between Athens and Sparta, Athens entered numerous teams into the Olympic chariot race, where they were extremely successful. Their victory distracted attention from the fact that Athens was being defeated in the war, proliferating the impression that everything was going well, which classics historian Paul Christesen described as "a straight-up geopolitical maneuver." A young Athenian politician named Alcibiades, who was responsible for bringing the chariot teams to compete at the Olympics, pivoted off his success, using it to hack a path toward war. In a speech in 415 BCE, he cited the recent Olympic victories as evidence of Athenian power and honor, imploring his compatriots to invade their rivals in Sicily.[38]

Many centuries later, Soviet powerbrokers who were aware of composer Dmitry Shostakovich's love of soccer tried to convert it into political wins. "Soviet authorities deployed [his] iconic status as well as his passion for the unimpeachably proletarian sport of football to further the purposes of propaganda," wrote Dmitry Braginsky. To be sure, Shostakovich played right into the politicization of his football-related creative work. His aforementioned ballet "The Golden Age" was a thinly veiled depiction of the football club Dynamo Moscow—the team sponsored by the Soviet Secret Police—and its sojourn to take on a Western team in a country called "Fascland" (the Fascist Land). The idea was that players on Dynamo Moscow "were actually class warriors, their true goal not just to win a sports competition but to destabilize or even destroy a capitalist country."[39]

FIFA (the *Fédération Internationale de Football Association*) was not always the cash vacuum that it is today. FIFA was founded in 1904 by a small group of soccer devotees from seven European countries who assembled in Paris to formalize the oversight of the sport and to create a set of common rules that would enable the global growth of the game. The original founders—hailing from Belgium,

Denmark, France, the Netherlands, Spain, Sweden, and Switzerland—chose Frenchman Robert Guérin to lead the organization as president. FIFA slowly expanded, bringing in British football associations, then soccer honchos from South Africa and eventually Latin America. The group decided to stage its first-ever World Cup in 1930 in Uruguay. Two years later, it set up headquarters in Zurich, Switzerland, where it remains today. In its entire history, FIFA has been helmed by only nine presidents, all men and all but one from Western Europe.

FIFA's rapid expansion and modernization occurred under the leadership of Englishman Sir Stanley Rous, president from 1961 to 1974. Rous took it upon himself to travel the globe to proselytize the gospel of soccer and to encourage the professionalization of both refereeing and coaching. He did so without pretension, surviving on his pension and allowing FIFA only to cover his travel expenses. Such modesty looks downright quaint compared to the approach of his successor, João Havelange, the Brazilian bus-company tycoon who was elected president of the organization in 1974, exploiting Rous's misguided support for South Africa's continued inclusion in FIFA, despite its racist apartheid policies, as his winning wedge. The geographical shift toward the Global South that Rous helped orchestrate, with membership burgeoning to 140 by the end of his tenure, led to his own undoing. Under Havelange, who ran the organization until 1998, soccer became big business, and with so much cash swishing through the system, corruption emerged as a serious issue. "The cronyism, the wheeling and dealing, the secret dubious deals, the nepotism, the lack of democracy and the abundance of dictatorial leadership" were all embedded in the wider soccer project under Havelange, notes David Yallop.[40]

FIFA's ambitions have long been in tension with its ethics. "The combination of rarely accountable leaders holding on to power alongside fragile principles vaguely sustaining the organizational infrastructure of the governing body have proved destabilizing throughout FIFA's history," writes soccer scholar Alan Tomlinson.[41] And yet, FIFA has not only survived, despite its manifest hypocrisies, but thrived. Today, it is the most powerful international sports federation on Earth, overseeing 211 member associations, outstripping the United Nations' 193 member states.

But when Uruguay hosted the first World Cup in 1930, FIFA was in its infancy. The tournament featured 13 teams and 18 matches. Uruguay President Juan Campisteguy attended all his country's matches, and his government covered all transportation and accommodation costs for visiting teams. The president was duly rewarded when Uruguay won the trophy. It was already clear that football—an emergent cultural force—could offer a political halo effect of sorts, both at home and abroad. This was part of a larger zeitgeist, and not all the beneficiaries were benign. As soccer historian David Goldblatt notes, "More finely attuned to the manipulation of popular taste, more ready and able to intervene in mass culture than the bumbling empires of *fin de siècle* Europe, the new dictators and populists of the 1920s and 1930s took a close and active interest in the game and there was no one to stop them."[42] The political use value of football was beginning to coalesce.

In light of the Eurocentrism that permeated FIFA at the time, selecting Uruguay to host might at first glance seem quizzical. But Uruguay had won the gold medal at both the 1924 Olympics in Paris and the 1928 Games in Amsterdam. Also, 1930 marked the centenary of Uruguay's independence from Spain. The FIFA president at the time, the Frenchman Jules Rimet, was enthusiastic at the prospect of bringing the inaugural tournament to Uruguay, as he detailed in his memoir *L'Histoire Merveilleuse des Coupes du Monde* (The Wonderful History of the World Cup). Rimet may well have fallen under the influence of Enrique

Buero—Uruguay's ambassador to Switzerland who doubled as a national soccer administrator—during long lakeside walks they shared in Geneva. This "South American coup," in the words of scholar Lorenzo Jalabert D'Amado, prefigured Havelange's crafty power-moves some decades later.[43] It also illuminates the throughline of personalized politics that wends through the entire history of the FIFA World Cup, from Rimet and Buero in the 1920s to Infantino and Trump a century later.

At the 1934 World Cup, soccer became a blunt instrument for advancing fascism. Although he was not a die-hard soccer aficionado, Benito Mussolini used the tournament to project a positive image of fascist Italy to a global audience and to convert the success of the Italian side, known as the *Azzurri*, into living, breathing prototypes of fascism's "New Man." This didn't emerge out of nowhere: Mussolini was an early adopter of sport as a mode of political manipulation. As early as 1928, the *New York Times* described an international football match between Italy and Czechoslovakia, staged in Rome, as signifying far more than sport for the fascists: "It is felt that the eleven athletes who take the field against the representatives of a foreign nation are engaging in a battle as vital to the country's interests as though it were an episode of a real war instead of a game." The article—titled "All Italy Focused on Football Game"—went on to assert, "Defeat would cast gloom over the whole country almost as if inferiority on the football field were indicative of the decaying virility and strength of the whole Italian people."[44]

Six years later, when Italy hosted the World Cup, such sentiments were amplified to a fever pitch. Ahead of the tournament, in order to represent itself to foreign tourists as a modern country, Italy built new stadiums, including one in Turin named after Mussolini and another in Florence named after the fascist martyr Giovanni Berta. To maximize audience, Under Secretary for Propaganda Galeazzo Ciano pressured the Italian press to place soccer on its front pages. Italian players were to be portrayed as "soldiers of sport," the fascist New Man incarnate.[45] The Italian Football Federation heavily subsidized the travel and accommodation costs for foreign fans and made sure that radio broadcasts of matches were transmitted to twelve of the sixteen competing countries, which did not include Uruguay, as the defending champions refused to travel to Italy, in part because they were cash strapped, but also because they felt snubbed by numerous European nations that refused to make the voyage to Latin America in 1930.

Mussolini turned the 1934 World Cup into a propaganda bonanza. "The greatest symbol of Mussolini's takeover of the World Cup was his introduction of the *Coppa del Duce* as a supplementary prize for the winner," writes Jonathan Wilson. "Sculpted in bronze, it depicted soccer players playing in front of fasces and stood six times taller than the Jules Rimet trophy."[46] Mussolini attended Italy's opening match alongside his sons and, amid a sea of fascist salutes, he watched the home side decimate the United States 7-1. After Italy defeated Czechoslovakia 2-1 in the final, Italy's coach Vittorio Pozzo and his squad grasped the *Coppa del Duce* and collected gold medals as well as autographed photographs courtesy of Il Duce himself. "The national anthems were played all over again," describes Goldblatt, "and Mussolini and the Fascist Party had their sporting paradigm of the nation's newfound strength."[47] Mussolini, a man known for riding a horse bare-chested—Putin-style—had hit the machismo jackpot. The Florence-based weekly *Il Bargello* claimed that the World Cup win was "the affirmation of an entire people, an indication of its virile and moral strength."[48]

This brand of virility and strength demanded perpetual flexing. After Italy's World Cup victory, Mussolini ramped up his aggressive foreign policy, invading Ethiopia in 1935 and intensifying his intervention in the Spanish Civil War in support of fellow fascist Francisco Franco. Il Duce connected the dots between sporting success and bellicosity.

"You athletes of Italy have particular duties," he said. "You must hence make use of all your energy and all your will-power in order to obtain primacy in all struggles on the earth, on the sea, and in the sky."[49] As with the full-blown sportswashing of the future, the popularity and power generated by those figurative "soldiers of sport" would scythe space for the all-too-real soldiers of war.

The year after Italy's World Cup victory, Avery Brundage—an up-and-coming sports administrator from Chicago and noted right-wing ideologue—wrote an essay for the *New York Times* that observed with more than a hint of appreciation that "Leaders representing such widely differing political philosophies as those of Mussolini, Hitler, and Stalin agree on the importance of sport and have initiated athletic programs designed to reach vast numbers."[50] Brundage was in the midst of a battle over whether to boycott the 1936 Olympics in Hitler's Berlin. Seeing the antisemitic writing on the German wall, groups like the National Association for the Advancement of Colored People, the American Jewish Congress, and the Non-Sectarian Anti-Nazi League argued in favor of boycotting. Brundage was adamantly opposed. In 1934, the American Olympic Committee (AOC) had sent Brundage on a fact-finding mission to Germany where, at the willing mercy of translators who fed him pro-Nazi disinformation, he warmed up to his German hosts, confiding at one point that he was a member of a private club in Chicago that excluded Jews. To no one's surprise, Brundage's "personal investigation" led him to the conclusion that Hitler and the Nazis would adhere to International Olympic Committee rules and not discriminate against visiting Jewish athletes. Upon his return to the United States, the AOC voted unanimously to attend the Games.[51]

The 1936 Berlin Olympics—what eventually became known as the Nazi Games—featured key elements of sportswashing. Adolf Hitler used the spectacle as a political launch pad. The Nazis even invented a special tradition that still exists today: the Olympic Torch Relay. Under their plan, a flame lit at Mount Olympus in Greece eventually wended its way to Berlin's Olympic stadium in the hands of hundreds of runners, where it ignited the Olympic cauldron. The relay—championed by Propaganda Minister Joseph Goebbels and ratified by the International Olympic Committee—traversed seven countries en route to Berlin. The path was strategic: not only did it spread the word about the upcoming Olympics, but it also allowed Hitler to circulate Nazi propaganda throughout central and southeastern Europe, prime zones of future Nazi geopolitical aspiration. During the final days of the relay, the regime exclusively chose blond and blue-eyed torch bearers, idealized exemplars of the Nazis' Aryan "master race."[52]

Journalists were entranced by the spectacle. A front-page *New York Times* story described Hitler as "the new Caesar of this era" who "was receiving the plaudits of a league far removed from politics, a league of peaceful sport to which he had become the proud host."[53] Another *New York Times* piece titled, "Olympics Leave Glow of Pride in the Reich," gushed that the Games galvanized "the undoubted improvement of world relations and general amiability." Olympic tourists couldn't help but leave Germany with the impression that "this is a nation happy and prosperous almost beyond belief; that Hitler is one of the greatest, if not the greatest, political leaders in the world today, and that Germans themselves are a much-maligned, hospitable, wholly peaceful people who deserve the best the world can give them." The journalist concluded, "Even if the Olympics have cost Germany 100,000,000 marks, most of which will go into the financial deficit, this has been a propaganda achievement well worth it."[54]

While the Olympics burnished Hitler's reputation abroad, it also gave him shine at home. The Führer's domestic popularity reached "its zenith in summer of 1936," notes Oliver Hilmes, "penetrating deep even into the working classes."[55] Strong domestic support laid the groundwork for military aggression. In the aftermath of the 1936 Olympics, Hitler swiftly turned his attention to waging invasions. Riding high after the Olympics, Hitler informed his military brass that the use of force would be required to realize Germany's destiny. The Olympic stadium was converted into a laboratory to develop technologies of war. In 1938, the country annexed Austria and occupied the Sudetenland. The *Kristallnacht,* or The Night of Broken Glass, unfolded in November 1938 when Nazis went on a violent rampage against Jews. In 1939, Germany claimed Czechoslovakia. By the end of that year—a mere three years after the Berlin Olympics—Europe was embroiled in World War II.[56] The core components of twenty-first-century sportswashing were taking shape.

The World Cup was weaponized once again in Argentina, where, in 1978, the ruling junta led by General Jorge Rafael Videla used the tournament to manufacture a thin veneer of consent. FIFA handed hosting duties to Argentina in 1966, long before the coup that installed the dictatorship that lasted from 1976 to 1983. During what became known as the "dirty war," the junta "disappeared" tens of thousands of leftists. Many were tortured in secret detention centers while others were dumped from airplanes—dead and alive—into the Atlantic Ocean. The US government was well aware of the atrocities. Declassified intelligence documents detail the "brutal methods employed by the military" and the "extensive use of torture" to crush dissent during the period. A summary by the US Assistant Secretary of State for Human Rights noted, "We continue to receive numerous highly credible reports that torture is used routinely in the interrogation of detainees." It added, "The electric 'picana,' something like a supercharged cattle prod, is still apparently a favorite tool, as is the 'submarine' treatment (immersion of the head in a tub of water, urine, excrement, blood, or a combination of these)." US officials concluded, "There is no longer any doubt that Argentina has the worst human rights record in South America." According to the Argentinian Commission for Human Rights, the disappearances continued during the World Cup, if at a decreased pace. In fact, a mere 700 meters from the River Plate Stadium—where Argentina defeated the Netherlands in the final 3-1—sat the *Escuela Superior de Mecánica de la Armada* (Naval Mechanics School), where some 5,000 "subversives" were brutally abused.[57]

And yet the World Cup continued on schedule. Former US Secretary of State Henry Kissinger, who attended the World Cup as a special guest of General Videla, certainly wasn't bothered. He attended Argentina's match against Peru, where Argentina needed to win by four goals to advance to the final. Before the match began, in an extremely unconventional move, Kissinger accompanied General Videla to Peru's locker room, where they wished the unnerved team luck and lectured them about Latin American solidarity and the brotherhood of football. Argentina went on to win 6-nil, with Peru opting to make an eyebrow-raising substitution of its star midfielder José Velásquez early in the second half when, at 2-0, the game was still in reach. Following the lead of Argentinian investigative journalist Maria-Laura Avignolo, who received numerous death threats for her efforts, David Yallop argues in *How They Stole the Game* that the game was fixed. General Videla's right-hand man, Captain Carlos Alberto Lacoste, allegedly arranged for a 35,000-ton shipment of grain to Peru and unfroze a $50 million credit line for the country, with additional bribes being shunted to various Peruvian administrators. Numerous players on Peru's squad reported being offered bribes.[58] Lacoste soon secured fast-tracked membership to FIFA where he worked as a faithful vice-president under João Havelange.

As Kissinger's five-day VIP tour concluded, he heaped praise on the junta. "The country I found is not the one advertised by the international press. Its situation is grossly misunderstood in Europe and the United States," opined the human-rights ogre. "The World Cup has projected an excellent image of Argentina toward the world. It's obvious that the country has made notable progress in a very short time frame."[59] Such image projection would become a key ingredient for sportswashing.

In *Long Distance Love: A Passion for Football,* Grant Farred argues that the 1978 World Cup in Argentina "forcefully demonstrated how a cultural moment can be not so much hijacked as deliberately structured by a repressive political regime." [60] The junta got an assist with its "deliberately structured" event from freshly enshrined FIFA president João Havelange. FIFA had allocated the World Cup to Argentina before Havelange assumed the FIFA presidency in 1974, but he was not troubled by the idea of an authoritarian junta presiding over the tournament. In an official FIFA report published in 1980, he described "the political and economic changes [Argentina] went through"—meaning the overthrow of a democratically elected government—as vital to making "a nearly perfect organization of the 1978 FIFA World Cup possible." In a 2010 interview in which he referred to the coup as "a revolution," he recalled, "One day I went to Buenos Aires. I was greeted by President Videla, and I told him, 'President, you have to make sure that you will do it, otherwise we will have to take action.' 'Mr. Havelange, I will not give you the best World Cup, but I'll give you one of the best World Cups. Don't worry.' And he gave it to me."[61]

The domestic press was largely compliant, with *La Prensa* running puff pieces featuring titles like, "Football Uniting Our Country and the Rest of the World in Brotherhood."[62] But the influx of international journalists covering the event was less predictable, leading the junta to rejigger its methods of political suppression. Just ahead of the tournament, before the foreign media arrived, state repression intensified in host cities, if more covertly. During the actual tournament, state suppression dwindled significantly, mirroring the arrival and work routines of foreign journalists. After the departure of foreign journalists at the tournament's conclusion, regime violence escalated once again.[63]

Thus, the fact that the global media spotlight swung onto Argentina for the World Cup created a fleeting opportunity for activism: the human-rights campaign orchestrated by *las Madres de la Plaza de Mayo* gained greater global visibility and was temporarily less repressible. As such, hosting the World Cup simultaneously bolstered the power of the ruling junta and revealed tactical fractures, a pattern that exists today. During the tournament, a transitory moment emerged in which debate over whether this was a "Dictatorship Cup" or a "World Cup of Peace" could transpire. Soccer writer Simon Kuper concluded, "The generals staged the World Cup to impress their own people and the world." However, in the end, it "was bad for investment and tourism in Argentina, and good for human rights."[64] And yet, for the first time, Coca-Cola signed on as a FIFA sponsor in 1978, starting a partnership that lasts through today. The 1978 World Cup helped firm up the corporate nature of the FIFA beast, pouring a firm fiscal foundation for sportswashing.

In the end, Argentinian journalist Ezequiel Fernández Moores concluded, "The 1978 World Cup was the most obvious political manipulation suffered by sport since the Olympic Games of 1936 in Nazi Germany."[65] But it would not be the last. Such "political manipulation" would be turbocharged by the tranche of cash that soon flowed into the global game. The man who was largely responsible for that rush of money was João Havelange.

"I can talk to any president and they'll be talking to a president too," said FIFA President João Havelange. "They've got their power and I've got mine: the power of football, which is the greatest power there is."[66] Part of Havelange's power derived from patronage. Unlike his predecessor Stanley Rous, Havelange covered the expenses of delegates from footballing nations around the world, arguing that doing so was an equalizer that would enable as many FIFA members as possible to participate in various meetings and congresses. Havelange also set up lavish spending accounts for FIFA members. Both changes in procedure ingratiated him with members and ensured their compliance. They also opened the door to eye-popping corruption.

Born to Belgian immigrants in Brazil, Havelange was an accomplished athlete who participated in the 1936 Olympics in swimming and 1952 Games in water polo. Havelange amassed power and prestige as head of the Brazilian Football Confederation. The man was known for his cold-blooded ruthlessness. According to one story from the 1982 World Cup, when Havelange realized that his 400 tickets for the Brazil-Russia match were not in the VIP section but instead located behind one of the goals, he directly confronted the man overseeing ticketing. When Havelange was told there were no remaining VIP tickets, he shut the windows, drew the blinds, slammed the door, and stated, "I can stay here for seventy-two hours without having a piss, shit, food, or sleep." Then he said to the man, who suffered from a heart condition, "You, on the other hand, might well die, because I am not going to let you leave until I have got my tickets in my hands." The FIFA boss walked out of the office with tickets in hand.[67]

Havelange clung doggedly to the canard that there was no place in sport for politics. At the same time, as Yallop points out, he "remained remarkably consistent throughout his life concerning the kind of people he prefers. Hitler and the Third Reich. The Brazilian Generals. Salazar's colleagues [in Portugal]. Banzer and the other members of the Bolivian junta."[68] Their autocratic tendencies chimed with his approach to leadership. After witnessing Havelange's iron-fisted negotiating style firsthand, Henry Kissinger remarked, "The politics of FIFA, they make me nostalgic for the Middle-East."[69]

Simultaneously, under Havelange, FIFA went full-throttle corporate. He formed a symbiotic relationship with Horst Dassler, head of Adidas. Through such multinational sponsorships as well as rising fees for World Cup broadcasting rights, Havelange was able to expand the tournament to twenty-four teams in 1982. In 1983, Dassler founded the sports marketing company International Sports and Leisure, setting up shop near FIFA's headquarters in Switzerland. For nearly two decades, the firm brokered television broadcasting and corporate sponsorship rights on behalf of FIFA, along the way funneling buckets of money in bribes and kickbacks to the FIFA president and his faithful minions. Many of the names that eventually appeared on the U.S. Department of Justice indictments in 2015 for alleged FIFA corruption were these very same sycophants and subordinates.

Under Havelange, the world's governing body for soccer not only became a brash corporatized money machine but also a second-rate development specialist, or, as scholar Alan Tomlinson put it, "a serious player in the remaking of the world order."[70] This "world order," grounded in grift and greed, would tee up an epic scandal that would rock the soccer world in 2015, right when sportswashing was in motion like never before.

4

Sportswashing and the World Cup in Russia and Qatar

Soccer honcho Chuck Blazer, who sat on FIFA's Executive Committee from 1996 to 2013, lived a lavish lifestyle on the forty-ninth floor of Trump Tower in Manhattan, where he reportedly maintained two apartments: an $18,000-a-month crash pad for himself, and a $6,000-per-month abode for his cats. On one hand, he was a one-of-a-kind, larger-than-life man, an eccentric known for transporting his 450-pound frame on a motorized scooter, zipping to and fro with a live parrot perched on his shoulder. On the other hand, the private jets, five-star accommodations, and bags of cash were just another Tuesday at FIFA. The US soccer powerbroker was eventually nabbed by the US Department of Justice on charges of bribery, money laundering, and tax evasion. Blazer chose to flip, becoming an informant and wearing a wire to secure admissions of guilt from his former colleagues over the corruption-drenched awarding of the 2018 and 2022 World Cups.[71]

FIFA's decision to hand the 2018 World Cup to Russia and the 2022 tournament to Qatar had long been shrouded in bribery allegations, emerging even before 2010, when FIFA staged its official vote. Blazer's damning testimony and his work as a snitch led to the Swiss authorities' 2015 raid at the five-star Baur au Lac Hotel in Zurich, where numerous FIFA officials were apprehended and marched away for questioning. Swiss prosecutors also raided FIFA headquarters, seizing damning documents and data. In addition, the Justice Department was looking into the allocation of the 2010 World Cup in South Africa and the 2011 election for FIFA president, won by João Havelange's successor Joseph "Sepp" Blatter. In the year following the raid in Zurich, dozens of people with links to FIFA were indicted, spanning every continent.[72] FIFA was a corruption-o-rama.

With so much money swirling through the FIFA system, perhaps it should come as no surprise that bribery was commonplace, if not compulsory. But under the influence of what the brilliant essayist Pankaj Mishra calls "moral self-entrancement," FIFA stepped across the line and got caught.[73] More than half the members of the FIFA Executive Committee who voted on hosting duties for the 2018 and 2022 World Cups were accused of corruption, even if many of them were not charged criminally. The Garcia Report, an investigation into the bidding process for the two tournaments led by lawyer Michael J. Garcia, concluded that irregularities in the voting process "were traceable to an Executive Committee culture of expectation and entitlement" kick-started by Havelange and extended by Blatter. Garcia added, "a number of Executive Committee members displayed a disregard for ethical guidelines and an attitude that the rules do not apply to them."[74] After his 2014 report was initially suppressed by the FIFA Ethics Committee, which instead published a summary exonerating Russia and Qatar from wrongdoing, it was ultimately released by FIFA in 2017, but only after the German newspaper *Bild* obtained a copy of the report and made plans to publish it. Despite the wide-ranging corruption scandal and FIFA's efforts to quash the truth, no smoking gun emerged that Russia and Qatar had bribed their way to hosting duties. The controversial World Cups remained firmly ensconced on global soccer's docket.[75]

Within a week of the 2015 raid in Zurich, Blatter had resigned, making way for Gianni Infantino, the head of UEFA (the Union of European Football Associations). The year after FIFA's corruption conflagration, the group implemented a set of much-ballyhooed reforms: instituting term limits for top leaders, disassembling the bloated committee system that fed FIFA's patronage machine, making public the votes for World Cup hosting rights, and allowing all

FIFA members—rather than just Executive Committee members—a vote. With some critics palliated, the juggernaut rolled on. And yet, ten years after the high-profile arrests of FIFA brass and their associates, the human-rights organization FairSquare issued a statement, signed by thirty-eight NGOs, whistleblowers, scholars, and writers (full disclosure: I was one of them), that insisted, "these reforms have failed to usher in a new era of responsible governance at FIFA and that the organization is structurally unfit to govern world football. FIFA is arguably more poorly governed today than it was 10 years ago."[76] This is the FIFA that will be gallivanting around North America for the 2026 World Cup, an organization that—under the trifecta of Havelange, Blatter, and Infantino—has become more and more autocratic.

Sportswashing activates multiple ping-points on the political infrastructure of global capitalism. It also thrives on illegality, ethics-free accumulation, personal enrichment, cults of personality. The Russia 2018 World Cup makes this crystal clear.

To mark the fact that Russia was hosting the 2013 World Youth Athletics Championships, the Sochi 2014 Winter

Olympics, and the 2018 World Cup, Vladimir Putin declared the 2010s as the country's "decade of sport." The Trump administration later repurposed this exact same slogan to connect events spanning the 2026 World Cup, the Los Angeles 2028 Summer Olympics, and the 2034 Winter Games in Salt Lake City.[77] For both Putin and Trump, the "decade of sport" framing suggested a sustained burst of success and provided them with an opportunity to look important on the world stage while the cameras rolled, to engage on positive terms with both international and domestic audiences, and to sharpen the hard edges of the security state.

The World Cup-induced political state of exception is a dictator's dream. The case of Russia spotlights how sportswashing can target a country's internal population as much as an international audience. Even when global audiences resisted Russia's greatness narrative, sportswashing jump-started national pride domestically and roused the feeling that the country was making political and economic progress.

From bid to delivery, World Cup organizers in Russia portrayed the event as an ambitious modernization project that transcended sport. The Russian president said in early 2018 that because of the World Cup, "We have created modern airports, train stations, roads, highway interchanges, and advancements in digital technologies and smart management systems" that will spur "the dynamic development of our regions, our cities, and the business activities of our country as a whole. And, of course, that it will improve the quality of life of our people."[78] This tapped into an underdog narrative that appealed to Russians domestically as well as international capital keen to advance into fresh terrains of profit. In Russia, the argument went, one could find low-wage laborers gaining new skills through hosting the World Cup. For potential investors, Russian leaders foregrounded that the nation was stable, dynamic, and primed for international integration. "World Cup organizers promoted Russia as a great nation, transitioning from a painful past into a fabulous future," writes Russia scholar Sven Daniel Wolfe. "And the World Cup would be part of that historic transition."[79]

Russian leaders calibrated a narrative for a domestic audience that it was under attack from the decadent West. "The anti-Russian campaign in the Western press is connected to the 2018 Football World Cup," warned a Ministry of Foreign Affairs official. "Soon, we will all witness active measures by the West ... they will take very serious actions in regards to Russia hosting this event. Of course, their goal is to disrupt it. They will use all information tactics available."

The bureaucrat concluded, "There will be many surprises... We are hurrying to counteract the PR campaign that prepares this informational trash."[80] Even principled criticism of Russia's invasion of Crimea was rebuffed as merely a Western disinformation campaign, lumped under the banner of outside agitators trying to undermine a proud Russian nation. This stoked both loyalty for the country and yearning for national strength. The ploy appeared to work. 62 percent of those polled in Russia were proud to host the 2018 World Cup and the Sochi 2014 Olympics.[81]

In the wake of the Sochi Games, Putin's approval rating soared to an all-time high of nearly 86 percent in May 2014.[82] This can partly be attributed to the fact that after the Olympics concluded and before the Paralympics commenced, Russia invaded the Crimean Peninsula, eventually annexing it from Ukraine. The "decade of sport" was paying geopolitical dividends. To an international audience, the Crimea invasion signified a rogue state. For the domestic audience inside Russia, it symbolized an unstoppable nation on the rise. Sportswashing with the brutal assist.

Putin's popularity also set the stage for the intensification of authoritarianism. Only two years after FIFA handed Russia the World Cup, the Kremlin, according to Human Rights Watch, "unleashed the worst political crackdown in Russia's post-Soviet history."[83] Journalists and activists were stifled through a series of repressive laws that curtailed access to public space. The government monitored social media, prosecuting people for posts critical of government policies, labeling them as "extremists" inciting hatred. In 2013, the Russian Duma passed a "gay propaganda" law targeting the LGBTQ community that outlawed the "promotion of nontraditional sexual relationships" to children. International visitors who broke the law faced deportation.[84] All this violated FIFA's Statutes as well as the organization's human-rights policy. And yet, FIFA remained quiet. They had a money spigot to protect, after all. In fact, one hundred days before the 2018 Russia World Cup kicked off, Infantino played football in the Kremlin with Putin.[85]

For the World Cup itself, Russia passed a law banning protests in host cities for the duration of the tournament.[86] The "diversity house" in St. Petersburg, designed to be a safe space for the LGBTQ community, was shuttered at the last minute, with the building's owners abruptly terminating the contract.[87] Russian authorities test-drove security technologies at the World Cup, normalizing repressive measures. They launched an invasive, digital Fan ID program, passport-sized badges draped on lanyards that fans needed to enter stadiums. To secure a badge, a raft of sensitive personal information was required—name, date of birth, home address, email addresses, phone numbers, passport numbers—and all of it was scooped up by Russia's Ministry of Communication. The fan identification program's use extended beyond the World Cup: it is now mandatory for attending domestic league matches. The Russian government has used it to target political activists. World Cup 2026 organizers are considering a similar system.[88]

Economically, Russia's "decade of sport" unfolded unevenly. The burst of spending on the Sochi 2014 Olympics occurred between 2010 and 2013 when Russia enjoyed relatively stable budgets amid declining growth. But the bulk of World Cup spending, which spanned 2015 to 2017, transpired amid a recession in Russia with dwindling budget revenues. Still, some throughlines exist. In both phases, Putin pushed what economist Peter Rutland calls a "new model of state-oligarchic capitalism," whereby state power trumped oligarchic wealth. Putin brought the "increasing fusion of state and oligarchic power" and the intensive renationalization of businesses after Boris Yeltsin's plutocratic bacchanalia of the 1990s, deploying unorthodox methods to mask the state's not-so-hidden hand.[89]

With ten of the twelve World Cup stadiums either built fresh or refurbished, there was plenty to plunder. Putin allotted massive World Cup contracts to close allies, using intimidation to signal to Russia's economic elites that their entitlement was wholly revocable, making it clear that oligarchs would be allowed to keep their billions on the condition they pony up millions to finance the mega-event spectacles.[90] This is a version of neopatrimonialism, described by Martin Müller and Sven Daniel Wolfe as "a system of governance with a pervasive network of patron-client relationships permeating and permeated by a legal-rational bureaucratic structure, wherein actors exchange loyalty for rents." For the 2018 World Cup this meant "rigged tenders for stadiums, prices inflated by contractors, the awarding of construction projects as political favors, and smokescreen public participation."[91] This all chimed mightily with FIFA's brand of clientelism grounded in fidelity though patronage, all orchestrated with scant public input.

At the opening match of the 2018 World Cup, Vladimir Putin sat in the presidential box alongside FIFA President Infantino and Mohammed bin Salman, the Crown Prince of Saudi Arabia, who was busy tilling the political soil for his own bid to secure football's marquee event. Putin also hosted disgraced former FIFA president Sepp Blatter as his personal guest, delivering a message of defiance to US prosecutors and FIFA brass alike. Riding high on the power of sportswashing, Putin capitalized by issuing an unpopular edict that raised the eligibility age for pensions, a clear attempt to smother the unpopular move beneath the excitement of the tournament at a time when protest was largely banned.[92]

As with the 1978 World Cup in Argentina, Russians reported that staging the tournament temporarily opened up space for public debate—and even protest—that was previously unthinkable.[93] Putin's underhanded pension shenanigans sparked sporadic street protests in cities not staging matches. Iranian women, banned from football stadiums in their home country, carried out protests at matches in Russia, donning banners emblazoned with the phrase, "Support Iranian Women to Attend Stadiums."[94] During the World Cup final, where France defeated Croatia 4-2, Pussy Riot—the feminist activist collective—pulled off a pitch invasion dressed as police personnel, dubbing it "performance art" meant to draw global attention toward Russian human-rights abuses. They were handed fifteen-day jail sentences and banned from attending sports matches for three years.[95]

Infantino touted Russia 2018 as the "best World Cup ever," and Putin returned the favor, bestowing the Order of Friendship medal upon the FIFA chief.[96] To the surprise of many, in 2022, four days after Russia invaded Ukraine, FIFA banned the country from all competitions. In early 2026, Infantino started hinting in public that Russia should be welcomed back into the FIFA fold.

Russia's "decade of sport" was "a tool for the Kremlin to achieve two goals," concluded scholars Vitaly Kazakov and Dmitrijs Andrejevs. "To showcase a 'new Russia' and impress domestic and international publics through spectacle and prestige, and to reduce resistance to the gradual introduction of authoritarian practices domestically and hostile geopolitical actions internationally."[97] This is the essence of sportswashing.

On the eve of the Qatar 2022 World Cup, FIFA President Gianni Infantino went on a rampage. During a rambling 57-minute screed that resembled an unhinged Trumpian "weave," Infantino suggested that his experiences as a son of Italian émigrés to Switzerland gave him preternatural powers of empathy. "Today I have very strong feelings," he began. "Today I feel Qatari. Today I feel Arab. Today I feel African. Today I feel gay. Today I feel disabled. Today I feel [like] a migrant worker." He eventually qualified his comments, saying he actually didn't belong to any of those groups, "But I feel like them, because I know what it means to be discriminated [against], to be bullied, as a foreigner in a foreign country. As a child at school I was bullied because I had red hair and freckles."[98]

Infantino then veered into smokescreen mode, dismissing the pervasive and well-documented concerns over worker abuse in the host country. “Qatar is actually offering them this opportunity. Hundreds of thousands of workers from developing countries come here, they earn ten times more than what they earn in their home country,” he rationalized. “And they do it in a legal way. We in Europe, we close our borders, and we don’t allow practically any worker from these countries who earn obviously very low income to work legally in our country, because we all know there are many illegal workers in our European countries.”[99]

Worker mistreatment during the preparations for the 2018 World Cup in Russia was appalling enough, but in Qatar, it reached an epic scale of heinousness. In Russia, unpaid wages and brutal working conditions were commonplace, with laborers toiling in minus twenty-five-degree Celsius temperatures without proper breaks. The Building and Wood Workers’ International reported at least seventeen deaths on World Cup stadium sites.[100] The football magazine *Josimar* revealed that 110 North Korean workers toiled on Zenit Arena in St. Petersburg under conditions so brutal that humanitarian groups described them as slavery.[101]

But worker exploitation ahead of the 2022 Qatar World Cup was even more ferocious. Amid the frenetic construction boom following FIFA's allocation of the tournament to Qatar, more than 6,500 migrant workers died. Around three dozen perished while working directly on World Cup stadiums. Workers brought to Qatar from countries such as Bangladesh, India, Nepal, Pakistan, and Sri Lanka under the exploitative kefala system—a migrant sponsorship program that can lead to forced labor—suffered mightily. Hundreds of thousands of migrant workers experienced grave abuse while helping Qatar prepare for the World Cup, and they did not receive financial compensation.[102] In 2024, FIFA's own Subcommittee on Human Rights and Social Responsibility determined that football's governing body was responsible for providing financial remedy to workers who were exploited in Qatar, using the 2022 World Cup legacy fund to do so. But FIFA promptly rejected the suggestion. Case closed.[103]

Qatar's constitutional monarchy, overseen by Amir Sheikh Tamim bin Hamad Al Thani since 2013, severely restricts free expression and assembly, so it was no surprise that when Abdullah Ibhais, a former media manager in Qatar's Supreme Committee for Delivery and Legacy for the World Cup, was detained in November 2019 after he questioned how Qatari authorities handled a migrant-worker protest against their unjust labor conditions. The Qatari government accused the Jordanian whistleblower of a wild array of charges, including bribery, misuse of state funds, and disclosure of restricted information that caused harm to the Supreme Committee. Ibhais denied all charges, but was found guilty and sentenced to five years in prison. He was released in March 2025. "For them, the World Cup—before anything else—was a reputational campaign that they spent more than 300 billion dollars to achieve," Ibhais later explained, spotlighting a key tenet of sportswashing.[104]

Somehow Gianni Infantino never managed to utter the words "Today I feel Abdullah Ibhais." In fact, Infantino relocated to Doha in autumn 2021, where he could more conveniently heap praise on Ibhais's oppressors: Nasser Al Khater, chief executive of the 2022 World Cup, and Hassan Al Thawadi, Secretary General of the Supreme Committee for Delivery and Legacy.[105]

Qatar is an oil-rich country specializing in natural gas and petroleum. To recirculate fossil-fuel capital, it undertook a methodical strategy of investing in sport far beyond its crown-jewel World Cup. A mere week after FIFA handed it the World Cup, FC Barcelona signed a $220 million sponsorship agreement with the Qatar Foundation, Doha's nonprofit development agency. That meant "Qatar Foundation" and later "Qatar Airlines" was emblazoned across the classic Barça kit—and thus worn by stars such as Leo Messi, Xavi Hernández, and Carles Puyol—creating a sporty halo effect for the Qataris. Then, the Qatar Investment Authority purchased legendary French club Paris St. Germain and spent billions to bring it to the apex of European football by adding stars like Kylian Mbappé, Neymar, and Ousmane Dembélé, all of them toiling with the Qatar Airways logo laced across their chests. Right in sync, Doha-based Al Jazeera paid $130 million a year to broadcast Ligue 1 matches in France. It also beamed hot properties such as the World Cup, Wimbledon, and the NBA across the Middle East. In addition, Qatar sponsored or hosted a surfeit of sporting events, such as the 2006 Asian Games, the 2011 Asian Cup soccer tournament, the Qatar Open Golf Masters, and the Qatar Open Tennis Tournament.[106] Qatar quickly became synonymous with high-level sports, softening the country's image in the eyes of billions around the world. This was soft power in action.

To appeal to a liberal global audience, Qatar World Cup organizers pitched the event as a beacon of environmental sustainability. In reality, this was a strident example of greenwashing: talking a big ecological game with little, if any, material follow-through. FIFA declared that the tournament was "a fully carbon-neutral event," a claim swiftly discredited by environmentalists who sniffed a greenwash from thousands of miles away (the same distance that the grass seeds flew on climate-controlled airplanes from the

United States to make the tournament's pitches). FIFA tabulated the carbon footprint for constructing seven new stadiums—many of which would become white elephants in the wake of the event—but underestimated emissions by a whopping factor of eight. Meanwhile, Qatar Energy, one of the world's biggest fonts of liquified natural gas, signed on as an official FIFA partner.[107] How a fossil-fuel sponsorship could be green, no one knew.

The debunked greenwash showed that sportswashing is a gamble with no guarantee of success. Efforts to sportswash can also invite increased scrutiny. Hosting the World Cup placed the unjust kafala labor system under the global microscope, and after relentless pressure from human-rights organizations, Qatar amended the system in 2020, becoming the first Gulf state to permit migrant workers to change posts—without their employer's permission—before their contracts ended. Qatar also set a minimum wage, although employers still maintained extraordinary control over migrant workers, many of them drowning in debt and living in perpetual fear of retribution. To be sure, Human Rights Watch reported that "passport confiscations, high recruitment fees, and deceptive recruitment practices are ongoing and largely go unpunished, and workers are banned from joining trade unions or striking." Still, these mild labor reforms would likely not have happened without pressure generated by the World Cup. Political pressure altered Qatar's sportswashing blueprints.[108]

The World Cup is wide open to grift and graft, entrenched as it is in the machinations of celebration capitalism, but it can also open up spaces of resistance. The unexpected star of the Qatar 2022 World Cup was Palestine, even though its team did not participate. Tunisian supporters unfurled an enormous "Free Palestine" banner at its match against Australia. Then, at Tunisia's match against France, a pitch invader darted across the turf carrying a Palestinian flag. Once he was apprehended by security, fans chanted, "Palestine!" as he was hauled away. Along Morocco's improbable route to the semifinals, its fans sang, "To our beloved Palestine, the most beautiful of all countries." After Morocco defeated Canada, players celebrated on-field with the Palestinian flag in hand. When the North African country defeated Spain in a penalty shootout to advance to the quarterfinals, players took their victory photo with a Palestinian flag.[109] As the Native Hawaiian political scientist Noenoe Silva writes, "But as power persists so does resistance, finding its way like water slowly carving crevices into and through rock."[110] Something to keep in mind as we pivot toward the 2026 World Cup.

5

The 2026 World Cup from Bid to Delivery: Controversies Arise

On the day of the 1994 World Cup opening match, organizers were hit with a massive distraction. Former NFL superstar O.J. Simpson was on the run from the law after being charged with the double homicide of his ex-wife Nicole Brown Simpson and Ron Goldman, hurtling down Interstate 5 in his white Ford Bronco while 95 million people watched on live television. In a letter that Simpson gave to his lawyer and friend Robert Kardashian (yes, those Kardashians) and published in the *New York Times* on the same day as the opening game between Germany and Bolivia, he wrote, "I think of my life and feel I've done most of the right things so why do I end up like this?"[111] Those who managed to bring the World Cup to the United States may have been feeling the same way. Just as their sporting spectacle was readying for lift-off, they were momentarily eclipsed by a star from the very sport that has long dominated the US sportscape, bumping soccer to the sidelines.

The tournament's opening ceremony was equally inauspicious. Partway through, Motown sensation Diana Ross emerged, sporting a bright red coat and matching slacks. But when Ross strode up, microphone in hand, to take a penalty kick, she accidentally slid off script, shanking her shot wide left. Nevertheless, per the stunt's original plan, the goal dramatically split in two, testing the suspension of disbelief among the 67,000 fans assembled at Chicago's Soldier Field (and millions more watching on television). Never could a better metaphor for the 1994 World Cup have been crafted: this was a spectacle that, no matter what happened on the field, was going to be a success for FIFA so long as success was measured in cold cash.

FIFA only staged the 1994 World Cup in the United States because João Havelange sniffed profit. After the Soviet Union disintegrated, he once told a journalist that only three major power blocs remained: the United States, FIFA, and the International Olympic Committee.[112] Now, two of them were teaming up to create a veritable money fountain. Nothing would stop them. When United States Soccer Federation President Werner Fricker started claiming money from marketing and broadcasting rights that were normally swallowed up by FIFA, Havelange bankrolled a candidate to replace him, with the subtext that a vote for Fricker was a vote for relocating the World Cup to another country. The

FIFA-approved candidate, Alan Rothenberg, joined the race only two weeks before the election. He won.[113]

The Havelange-Rothenberg partnership yielded enormous profits, at least for FIFA. FIFA sponsors anted up around $300 million to cozy up to the much-coveted US consumer, while licensed World Cup goods netted another billion. The tournament broke attendance records, selling more than 3.5 million tickets. The final between Brazil and Italy was watched by nearly 95,000 in Pasadena with an average ticket price of $460 ($1,009 in 2026 dollars).[114]

FIFA honcho Sepp Blatter often claimed that the tournament generated $4 billion in revenues. But for whom did the 1994 World Cup boom? Turns out the tournament was a classic case of trickle-up economics, with profits leaking from local host communities and into the bank accounts of FIFA and its corporate partners. Independent academic economists found that fiscal success for host cities was largely mythical. Their evidence suggested that "the World Cup had *an overall negative impact* on the average host city and the US economy overall," with $9.26 billion in *losses* from hosting tournament matches. A handful of cities ended up making money, but nine of the thirteen host metropolises—including Los Angeles, San Francisco, and New York—hemorrhaged cash.[115]

For his eager-beaver compliance, Rothenberg was duly rewarded by FIFA. He was handed a $3 million bonus to go along with his $4 million in base pay. Thanks to his five-year contract, he would continue to collect $800,000 a year through 1996, two full years after the tournament concluded. As Yallop dryly noted, "Ten thousand unpaid volunteers who had worked day and night to make the event were not asked either individually or collectively for an opinion on Alan I. Rothenberg." The FIFA kingmaker machine had rolled another grifting princeling off its gold-plated conveyor belt.[116] Rothenberg used his clout to forge Major League Soccer (MLS), the US professional league that protects the billionaire owner class by refusing to institute a promotion-relegation system like the rest of the world's top-shelf football divisions. MLS is "not *quite* a Ponzi scheme," notes sports economist Neil deMause, since "there's light at the end of the revenue tunnel beyond just finding new suckers" to pay exorbitant fees to secure expansion teams.[117]

That's not to say the 1994 World Cup itself failed to deliver drama. Oprah Winfrey emceed the opening ceremony, at one point inadvertently falling off the stage. Argentinian soccer legend Diego Maradona—known for his magical left foot, his principled leftist politics, and his "Hand of God"—was disqualified from the tournament after failing a drug test. The host country had a decent showing, upsetting

Colombia, a country among the oddsmakers' favorites. (Later that year, Andrés Escobar, the Colombian defender who knocked in an own goal for the United States, was gunned down in the parking lot of a Medellín nightclub.) In the final, after 120 goal-less minutes, Italy's pony-tailed talisman Roberto Baggio missed his penalty kick, smashing it over the bar and providing an almost mystical symmetry with Diana Ross's botched pen at the opening ceremony. Brazil walked away with the Jules Rimet trophy. Raí Oliveira captained the *Seleção* during the group stage. Like his older brother Socrates, Raí was an eminently political footballer. Decades later, he'd call out Brazilian President Jair Bolsonaro's authoritarian tendencies. In 2025, Bolsonaro was sentenced to twenty-seven years in prison for plotting a coup. Meanwhile, his staunch ally in the United States, who sanctioned another failed coup of sorts, the January 6 attack on the Capitol in 2020, remained free to fashion an extraordinary sportswash.

Under Infantino, FIFA has embraced its inner glutton, gorging its cash-cow tournament with abandon. The 1994 World Cup included 24 teams and 52 matches, whereas the 2026 tournament will be twice as big, with 48 teams and

104 matches. By comparison, the previous World Cup in Qatar in 2022 featured only 32 countries and 64 matches. With the 2026 World Cup, FIFA aims to shatter the 1994 tournament's attendance record of 3.5 million people. FIFA also hopes to gobble up $13 billion in the four-year budget cycle (2023-2026), more than $11 billion of that through the 2026 World Cup alone, making it the most lucrative event in the history of sports.[118]

The "United 2026 bid" for the World Cup—put forth in 2017 by the United States, Canada, and Mexico—feels like it was forged from another era than the one plaguing us in 2026. The bid's introduction stated, "Canada, Mexico, and the United States are more than neighbors, we are partners. We share borders and values." It added, "We call ourselves the United Bid because we are truly approaching this challenge together—UNITED, AS ONE." The bid team also claimed, "Together with FIFA, we will work tirelessly to deliver a FIFA World Cup™ of the highest standards" (with a tactical "TM" to nod to the fact that FIFA is the notoriously litigious owner and operator of the event), promising an "inclusive" tournament "that embeds respect for human rights and respect for fundamental freedoms and values at its core."[119]

The full slogan in the bid materials was "Unity. Certainty. Opportunity." But with an erratic Trump at the helm—his worst instincts stoked by the fawning FIFA president—the enterprise is anything but certain. Since FIFA granted the trio hosting rights in 2018, choosing the United 2026 bid over Morocco by a one-vote-per-nation tally of 134 to 65, Trump has instigated full-throttle turbulence, especially in his second term, threatening to annex Canada as the fifty-first state and to send in the military to attack drug cartels on Mexican land. He instituted a travel ban that bars fans from at least four qualified nations from attending the tournament: Haiti, Iran, Ivory Coast, and Senegal. Trump wields disproportionate influence over the shape and tenor of the event, but it already leaned unmistakably in the direction of the trio's hegemon, with 78 matches in the United States and only 13 apiece in Canada and Mexico. Ever the blowhard, Trump said the quiet part out loud at the August 2025 announcement that the World Cup draw would take place in Washington, DC: "We did a little for Canada. We did a little for Mexico … See, I'm a good citizen. I said, 'Let them have a little piece.' So we gave a little to Canada. See how nice I am? And we gave a little bit to Mexico."[120]

The United 2026 bid vowed that it "fully commits to respecting human rights in all aspects of our work before, during, and after" the World Cup "in accordance with the UN Guiding Principles on Business and Human Rights." Bidders assured FIFA, "Our commitment embraces all

Internationally Recognized Human Rights," and listed numerous human-rights standards it would supposedly abide, including the International Bill of Human Rights—made up of the Universal Declaration of Human Rights, the International Covenant on Civil and Political Rights, and the International Covenant on Economic, Social and Cultural Rights—as well as the core principles in the International Labor Organization Declaration on Fundamental Principles and Rights at Work.[121] A collection of human-rights and labor groups—including the ACLU, AFL-CIO, Amnesty International, Athlete Ally, Human Rights Watch, the Independent Supporters Council, NAACP, Reporters Without Borders, and the Sport and Rights Alliance—raised alarm bells in December 2025. "The 2026 World Cup is the first to begin with human rights criteria embedded in the bidding process. But the deteriorating human rights situation in the United States has put those commitments at risk," said Andrea Florence, the Brazilian lawyer and executive director of the Sport and Rights Alliance.[122] Still, the FIFA juggernaut rolled on.

To juice the bid, Trump penned three letters to FIFA in early 2018, attempting to convince the group to hand over 2026 World Cup hosting duties. Citing past instances of the US staging World Cups and the Olympics, he wrote, "I am confident that the United States would host the 2026

FIFA World Cup in a similarly open and festive manner, and that all eligible athletes, officials, and fans from all countries around the world would be able to enter the United States without discrimination."[123] As if to hedge their bets, the bid team emphasized to FIFA voters that Trump's second term would end before the World Cup. Little did they know that his second term would begin in 2025, not 2021.

Bid documents for sports mega-events like the World Cup and Olympics are infamous for being loaded with false promises. But the chasm between word and deed in the United 2026 bid is downright jaw-dropping. When the US started bombing Iran in February 2026, a mere 107 days before the Islamic Republic's first match, it marked the first time that a World Cup host had attacked another participating nation in advance of the tournament. (England had been in bloody skirmishes with Borneo and Aden—neither were part of the tournament—when it hosted the World Cup in 1966, but this was on another level.) The brutality was bracing. The US bombed a school, killing dozens of girls in Hormozgan province. Dozens more people were massacred when a US bomb struck a sports hall in Fars province.[124] The Trump administration engaged in political assassination in broad political daylight, targeting Iran's supreme leader Ayatollah Ali Khamenei and other top officials. When asked afterwards whether he thought

Iran would be able to participate in the 2026 World Cup, Trump responded, "I really don't care," adding, "I think Iran is a very badly defeated country."[125] Infantino's response? One could say crickets, but crickets actually make noise.

In March 2026, Iran's sports minister announced that Iran would not attend the World Cup: "Considering that this corrupt regime has assassinated our leader, under no circumstances can we participate in the World Cup."[126] Then Trump posted a veiled threat on social media, further throwing Iran's participation into question: "The Iran national soccer team is welcome to the World Cup, but I really don't believe it is appropriate that they be there, for their own life and safety."[127]

It's instructive to look at how FIFA assessed the United 2026 and Morocco bids, as it reveals the group's true motives and values. In addition to evaluating basic must-haves such as stadiums, transportation systems, and hotel availability, FIFA takes great care to carry out a "tax assessment" for each bid. This is code language for tax exemptions, which have become an integral element of the FIFA grift machine. After reviewing the lopsided contracts between FIFA and the South African government for the 2010 World Cup, attorney Sophie Nakueira depicted the world's governing body as a "floating sovereign."[128] In other words, FIFA is a parastate that acts like a parasite, treating World Cup hosts like its own private buffet.

In its "Bid Evaluation Report" for the United 2026 and Morocco bids, FIFA included a special category for rating each country's willingness to offer massive tax exemptions for both media and marketing. Assessing Morocco's unsuccessful bid and the United 2026 winning bid, FIFA gave its highest ratings to Morocco and Mexico (in the pre-President Claudia Sheinbaum era) for their willingness to offer a "full tax exemption." The US assured FIFA of a "full tax exemption" for media and a "close-to-full tax exemption" for marketing revenues, while Trump supplied a letter in 2018 suggesting fiscal guarantees that seemed to settle any jitters that might have been tingling in FIFA's collective spine. Canada, meanwhile, played hardball with taxpayer funds and earned a—womp-womp—"limited tax exemption" rating in both areas.[129] Although the tournament ends in July 2026, FIFA somehow requires that its tax exemptions last through December 31, 2028.[130]

Nick McGeehan, the director of the human-rights group FairSquare, told me, "Tax exemptions allow FIFA to suck vast amounts of money out of its hosts. The majority of the cost of preparing the tournament falls on the hosts, while FIFA pockets all the revenue that is generated from the sale of broadcasting and marketing rights." McGeehan added, "FIFA demands tax exemptions on all of this money and for the revenue generated by many of its partners too."[131] This includes some of the wealthiest media and marketing firms on the planet.

Acquiring specific information about FIFA's tax breaks is a gumshoe affair involving obscure government and FIFA documents. The task is complicated by the fact that FIFA created individualized contracts with each of the eleven US host cities—unlike the 1994 World Cup, when a centralized organizing committee oversaw the contract for all host metropolises—thereby splintering liability and gifting FIFA with an opportunity to achieve the maximum squeeze on a city-by-city basis. [132] Inter-city solidarity be damned. FIFA-imposed ironclad secrecy rules.

FIFA's coffers are stuffed full. As previously noted, over the 2023-2026 cycle alone, FIFA is projected to rake in $13 billion, including $4.26 billion in television broadcasting rights, $3.1 billion in hospitality rights and ticket sales, and $2.7 billion in licensing rights.[133] Its Tier 1 FIFA "Partners" include some of the world's most powerful corporations: Adidas, Aramco, Coca-Cola, Hyundai-Kia, Lenovo, Qatar Airways, and Visa. They hold global rights over all FIFA competitions.[134] In Spring 2024, FIFA signed a deal with Aramco—Saudi Arabia's state-owned fossil-fuel behemoth—that's reportedly worth $100 million per year.[135] Tier 2 "Sponsors" acquire global rights for a specific edition of the World Cup and for 2026 include AB InBev (Budweiser), Bank of America, Lay's, Hisense, McDonald's, Mengniu Dairy, Unilever, and Verizon. These deals tend to fall in the $65 million to $95 million range. The Tier 3, "Regional Supporters and Suppliers," includes Airbnb, American Airlines, Diageo, Home Depot, Marriott Bonvoy, Rock-It Cargo, DoorDash, Globant, Boggi Milano, and Valvoline.[136] FIFA's phalanx of lawyers offers these corporations monomaniacal brand protection from ambush marketers. Less than one hundred days before the tournament kicked off, FIFA announced yet another money stream, allowing commercials to run during the "hydration breaks" that it instituted halfway through each half of every match.[137] Even the effects of climate change seem to boost FIFA's bottom line.

To be sure, FIFA insists it redistributes its spoils, reinvesting to grow the game and to buoy its 211 member associations around the world. For the 2026 World Cup, FIFA is handing out $655 million to participating teams, with the champions walking off with $50 million and the runners-up $33 million. Third place nets $29 million while fourth place receives $27 million. Teams that fall in fifth to eighth place get $19 million, whereas ninth to sixteenth place receive $15 million. Those who make it out of the group stage but lose in the first round take home $11 million, while countries that fail to advance out of their group nab $9 million.[138]

Some of those winnings derive from a new FIFA trick. World Cup tickets that are resold in the United States and Canada will be based on "dynamic pricing," which allows FIFA to nimbly jack up ticket prices based on demand—similar to when a rideshare app increases its price during inclement weather. In the US and Canada, no cap exists on the price of tickets being resold (whereas in Mexico, resale laws are stricter, limiting resale prices to the face value of the ticket). Moreover, FIFA claims a hefty 15 percent chunk of all resold tickets *from both the seller and the buyer*. In other words, FIFA is incentivizing the worst instincts of ticket scalpers and ticket-touting scoundrels of all stripes.[139] When comedian John Oliver called FIFA "a criminal organization," this is exactly why.[140]

Enter Zohran Mamdani, the Mayor of New York who, as part of his insurgent campaign, targeted FIFA's profiteering. He launched a "Game Over Greed" initiative that slammed FIFA for pricing out most New Yorkers from attending the World Cup, echoing his mantra that the city faces a crisis of affordability. Mamdani—an avid soccer fan and longtime supporter of Arsenal FC of the English Premier league—demanded that FIFA "put game over greed," cease dynamic pricing, abolish resale markets with no caps, and set aside 15 percent of its tickets for local residents.[141] After all, at previous World Cups, including Qatar 2022, FIFA earmarked tickets for low-income locals.[142] The miniscule portion of "Supporter Entry Tier" $60 tickets that FIFA is hyping for the 2026 World Cup is a cruel joke.[143] Perhaps it shouldn't come as a surprise that in the hyper-capitalist United States, FIFA is pushing its extractivist greed machine to new outer limits.

Price gouging is only one among many controversies plaguing the 2026 World Cup. Numerous cities are in open rebellion over having to bear the fiscal risks, while FIFA scoops up the rewards. Residents across North America are bracing for extra costs related to security and logistics. In the United States, the so-called One Big Beautiful Bill Act, passed in summer 2025, allocated $625 million for "security and other costs related to the Fifa World Cup," but local leaders are concerned that costs in the neighborhood of "$150 million per city" will fall on the shoulders of local taxpayers.[144] At the same time, Trump is weaponizing the

World Cup by threatening to withdraw hosting duties from US cities with outspoken Democratic mayors, such as Seattle and Boston.[145] Numerous fan fests—public spaces where football fans can experience the joy of the event without forking over exorbitant ticket fees—are either being canceled or scaled back.[146] For those who actually can afford a ticket to a match in Los Angeles, they can also expect to pay $300 for parking.[147] Only the one-two punch of Trump and FIFA "could squeeze every bit of fun out of the Cup," wrote Dave Zirin in *The Nation*.[148]

Meanwhile, in Canada, the World Cup is skewing public priorities. Amid layoffs in Vancouver's city government, World Cup planning remains unaffected. "It's a contractual obligation" with FIFA, explained a deputy city manager. "We have no wiggle room in terms of delivering what we need to deliver." At the same time, the leader of Vancouver's local organizing committee, Jessie Adcock, hauled in a whopping $470,000 in 2024 alone, more than doubling the British Columbia Premier David Eby's salary of around $227,000. "Vancouver's involvement in FIFA 26 lacks any credible, publicly available business case, only rosy government news releases with a variety of cost ranges, revenue estimates and aspirations of a future tourism legacy," Canadian journalist Bob Mackin told me. "There is no effort to mitigate the harms to the people struggling in the community."[149] Across the country in Toronto, to the horror of local activists, a warming center for unhoused residents was shut down a month early so that FIFA could set up a staging area.[150] It's no wonder that soccer-mad cities like Chicago and Minneapolis said thanks but no thanks to hosting matches.

Sports mega-events like the World Cup also create a pretext for security forces to test-drive new and invasive technologies. When the inaugural match of the 2026 World Cup—featuring Mexico versus South Africa—takes place on June 11 in front of an 83,000 people at Estadio Azteca, it will be patrolled by robot dogs on the ground and drones in the sky. The robot dogs operate semi-autonomously and are equipped with video cameras and night vision. The drones are controlled by portable units that look like high-tech rifles. All three Mexican host cities—Guadalajara, Monterrey, and Mexico City—will be jam-packed with security personnel, some 100,000 in total from the military, the country's Security Ministry, and private security firms.[151] At the 2026 World Cup, the line between sporting event and police convention will become ever blurrier, normalizing the intensification of militarized policing along the way.

On top of all this, a specter is haunting the 2026 World Cup: an out-of-control US Immigration and Customs Enforcement, or ICE. The World Cup final has been designated a National Special Security Event, and the NSSE that Biden instituted in 2024 is still in effect in Los Angeles, so numerous federal security and intelligence agencies will have extraordinarily wide latitude in which to carry out Trump's racist deportation fever dream.[152]

Trump administration officials have been clear that ICE will police the World Cup. JD Vance raised a million hackles in May 2025 when he "joked" that World Cup tourists better not overstay their visas or they'd be snapped up by ICE goons. He said, "I know we'll have visitors probably from close to 100 countries. We want them to come. We want them to celebrate. We want them to watch the game. But, when the time is up, they'll have to go home. Otherwise, they'll have to talk to [then-Department of Homeland Security] Secretary [Kristi] Noem." Nothing quite like a veiled threat to ship visiting soccer fans to El Salvador's notorious CECOT torture camp to get the yuks a-flowing or to prime the tourist profit pump.[153]

But more serious voices reinforced Vance's core message: the United States is not a safe place for tourists to watch soccer. ICE's Acting Director Todd Lyons stated in February 2026, precisely four months before the tournament kicked off, that ICE will be a "key part" of the security infrastructure at this year's men's World Cup. More specifically, Homeland Security Investigations—whose presence at the 2026 Milano Cortina Winter Olympics galvanized street protests and fiery condemnation from Milano's mayor—will be on the ground at the World Cup.[154] This echoed the comments of failson Andrew Giuliani—the executive director of the White House Task Force for the FIFA World Cup 2026—who, when asked whether ICE would be detaining immigrants at matches, responded, "the President does not rule out anything that will help make American citizens safer."[155]

This followed countless harrowing stories of masked ICE agents brutally detaining US citizens, green-card holders, and undocumented people. Even Native Americans are being scooped up by ICE at alarming rates. Navajo Nation president Buu Nygren recounted how numerous Navajo citizens have experienced "negative and sometimes traumatizing encounters" with ICE. If the out-of-control crackdown—orchestrated by ICE and the US Customs and Border Patrol—is imperiling this country's First Peoples, then you can bet it is dangerous for visitors from around the world. Ask the teenage backpackers from Germany who reported being strip-searched and imprisoned after landing in Hawaii. Ask the Canadian entrepreneur who spent two weeks in the Otay Mesa Detention Center, an experience she depicted as being "kidnapped, thrown into some sort of sick psychological experiment meant to strip us of every ounce of strength and dignity." Ask green-card holder, lawful permanent resident, and Columbia University student Mahmoud Khalil.[156] Ask those killed by ICE. Ask Renée Good. Ask Alex Pretti. Ask Ruben Ray Martinez. This list goes on.

Ahead of the World Cup, the Trump regime is constructing "mega detention centers" while willfully conflating activists and terrorists and constructing a "domestic terrorism" watchlist. Indefinite detention and family separation are commonplace, as is the presence of the military on the streets of US cities. "We've seen rapid normalization of abuses we once associated with authoritarian regimes or the old Iron Curtain countries," wrote policing expert Radley Balko. "It's now routine for masked, unidentifiable government agents to sweep people off the street and whisk them away in unmarked vehicles" to detention facilities far away without notifying their lawyers or families. Some are even sent to third countries where they have no ties whatsoever. People are also being "explicitly targeted for their political opinions, their activism, or their journalism."[157]

This is the grim context in which the 2026 World Cup will transpire. And the world has taken notice. Tourism to the United States has plummeted. The German football club Werder Bremen canceled plans to travel to Minnesota and Michigan for friendly matches, citing ICE brutality and potential immigration woes: "Playing in a city where there is unrest and people have been shot does not fit with our values," a club spokesperson said. "Furthermore, it was unclear to us which players would be able to enter the USA at all due to the stricter entry requirements."[158] It's probably time to listen when the Germans are telling you that your country is getting too authoritarian.

Concerns over fan safety are emerging in the strangest of places. When asked about the European Sports Commissioner's concern over ICE's role in World Cup security, former FIFA President Sepp Blatter said, "The EU sports commissioner's concern is justified. Given the politically unstable situation and the security conditions in the United States, this tournament must be critically questioned." Blatter added, "What happened in Minneapolis is worse than anything that ever happened in Qatar, which hosted the 2022 World Cup."[159]

Global soccer fans are also alarmed by the Trump administration's proposal to collect the social-media posts and enormous amounts of personal information of visitors from several dozen countries that enjoy visa-free travel to the United States, including numerous World Cup participants that are traditional US allies: Australia, Austria, Belgium, Croatia, England, France, Germany, Japan, Netherlands, New Zealand, Norway, Portugal, Qatar, South Korea, Spain, and Switzerland. According to the proposal, visitors from these countries are required to submit extraordinarily invasive "high value data" that includes the most recent five years' worth of their social-media activity; all telephone numbers from the last five years; all email addresses from the last ten years; electronically-submitted photos replete with metadata and IP addresses; the names, dates of birth, places of birth, and telephone numbers of family members such as parents, spouse, siblings, and children. Biometrics would also be mandatory, including DNA samples, face scans, iris scans, and fingerprints. At the time of writing, the proposal was in the midst of a public-comment period.[160]

Perhaps, as we saw with previous World Cups in Argentina, Russia, and Qatar, the repression will temporarily slow down. But Trump is extremely erratic—to make a severe understatement—so you never know.

In the twenty-first century, nothing shapes political culture and values quite like the sports industrial complex, entrenched as it is in the spheres of high technology, securitization, and entertainment. As the most lucrative sports event ever, the 2026 World Cup is the crown jewel of Trump's exploitation of sports for political gain. "Football is always telling you things about the world," noted *Guardian* columnist Barney Ronay, "always running ahead to the tide."[161] As we will see in Chapter 6, Trump has lined up the sportswashing dominoes to fall in his economic direction. And Gianni Infantino, FIFA's grifting quisling and Trump's human colonoscopy volunteer, is doing everything in his power to help. But there are activist groups afoot who intend to use the tournament to raise vital social issues into public consciousness, to coordinate fightback.

6

The World Cup, Sportswashing, and Activist Fightback

"FIFA is a dictatorship!"

One might expect this exclamation to fly from the mouth of an activist. Or maybe a construction worker who experienced extreme exploitation amid preparations for the World Cup in Russia or Qatar. Or perhaps a resident of Switzerland, exasperated with FIFA for taking advantage of their country as a cushy tax haven. But no, this outburst was actually from former FIFA President Sepp Blatter less than four months before the 2026 World Cup kicked off, slamming his successor Gianni Infantino for running football's global governing body like a fiefdom. Blatter wasn't done. "Who is FIFA today?" he asked. "It consists only of its president, Infantino." When asked whether Infantino might be playing a long game, buddying up to Trump to eventually exert influence over his most nefarious proclivities during the World Cup, Blatter replied, "I have not heard or read of a single occasion on which Infantino stopped Trump from doing anything—even though his policies cry out to heaven." He curtly, and correctly, described Infantino's relationship with Trump as "submissive."[162]

To be sure, Blatter is no paragon of integrity. Not only was he in charge of FIFA during its biggest corruption scandal back in 2015, but he's also the same guy who thought on-field racism could be settled with a mere handshake.[163] At the 2014 World Cup draw, he interrupted a minute of silence for Nelson Mandela after less than ten seconds.[164] He once made the sexist suggestion that women footballers should wear "tighter shorts" in order to attract fans and "to create a more female aesthetic." In response, Norwegian footballer Lise Klaveness retorted, "If the crowd only wants to come and watch models then they should go and buy a copy of Playboy."[165]

Klaveness went on to play more than seventy matches for Norway's national team before eventually becoming the president of the Norwegian Football Association in 2022. In that capacity, she has been one of the fiercest critics inside the upper echelons of global football. She excoriated football's higher-ups for failing to take seriously the plight of either migrant workers or the LGBTQ community in World Cup host Qatar. Klaveness called for UEFA to consider excluding Israel from international soccer competitions over its human-rights atrocities in Gaza and the West Bank. "None of us can remain indifferent to the disproportionate attacks that Israel has subjected the civilian population in Gaza to," she said.[166]

Ahead of the 2026 World Cup, which will include Norway for the first time since 1998, Klaveness had thoughts about Donald Trump's clear-cut sportswash. "Recently I sat in Washington, in a room full of football presidents, and felt the painful feeling of being hostage to something that is obviously wrong," she said. "The feeling that the emperor is not only walking without clothes—but that he is leading us in a dangerous direction, and that at the same time I cannot stop it. Not there and then, at least."[167] No single person can stop the Trump-Infantino sportswashing juggernaut; like all battles against entrenched power, it would take a strategic, committed movement to put a dent in the FIFA machine. Across North America, activists are revving up for just such a David-versus-Goliath fight.

Any protest against the 2026 World Cup faces an uphill battle. Soccer is the world's most popular sport, and with rising fascism roiling the globe, many fans quite reasonably desire a respite from the political mayhem, as fanciful as that may be. Yes, the World Cup braids political, economic, and cultural power into a stiff bullwhip that can be used to silence dissent. But we're at a pick-a-side juncture in history, and the 2026 World Cup offers a moment to choose the right one.

For Trump, sports are more important than ever. Even before the Trump regime's seismic incompetence and imperial incoherence against Iran in spring 2026, the unraveling of the neoconservative fever dream in the Middle East and beyond had "for all practical purposes resulted in the terminal crisis of US hegemony—that is, in its transformation into mere domination," wrote noted world-systems analyst Giovanni Arrighi in 2010.[168] The Biden and Trump administrations' diehard support of Israel as it executes genocide against Palestinians only solidifies the historical shift from a reliance on soft-power enticement to hard-power cudgel. In teaming up with Israel to wage war on Iran only months before the 2026 World Cup, Trump not only replicated the worst atrocities and strategic blunders of Dick Cheney-brand neoconservatism, but also doubled down on the necessity to cling to sports.

With twenty-first-century sportswashing, political leaders are using soccer as a launch pad for personal and national enrichment, and they do not take kindly to those who get in their way. Exhibit A: Donald Trump is teaming up with Saudi Arabia for a sportswash in multiple acts.

Trump has an avid sportswashing partner in Mohammed bin Salman, the Crown Prince of Saudi Arabia. To sportswash, Saudi Arabia uses its Public Investment Fund to activate its oil wealth and diversify its investment portfolio while simultaneously shining up its global image. Research by Stanis Elsborg and Karim Zidan documents Saudi Arabia's ever-widening sport footprint. Their report "Saudi Arabia's Grip on World Sports" unearths more than 900 sponsorships and 1,400 strategic arrangements that the Gulf state has taken to sportswash its global image. Saudi Arabia has invested in a dizzying array of sporting projects, from purchasing Newcastle United in the English Premier League to funding LIV International Golf to pumping up its domestic football Saudi Pro League.[169]

Riyadh's sport-driven propaganda is designed to amend perceptions of Saudi Arabia, both externally—in the countries where their teams and events plant roots—and domestically, where Saudis can feel pride in their country as an emergent global power player and cultural influencer. Their sportswashing is also meant to deflect attention from an array of depredations, such as the 2018 killing of *Washington Post* journalist Jamal Khashoggi in the Saudi consulate in Istanbul, Turkey, his body hacked into chunks with a bone saw before being discreetly discarded, with many alleging the assassination was directed by bin Salman himself. Beyond this, women's rights advocates in Saudi Arabia are routinely suppressed while the country oversees mass executions and metes out inflated prison sentences to peaceful activists. There's also the country's brutal bombing and domination in Yemen.[170]

But sportswashing requires willing partners. FIFA, the United States, and Saudi Arabia form a key nexus that clarifies the political and economic benefits of sportswashing for national, organizational, and personal enrichment. In December 2024, after a suspiciously expedited bidding process, FIFA named Saudi Arabia as host of the 2034 World Cup. It was a sportswasher's dream come true.

The decision paid quick dividends. The following year, FIFA and the Saudi Fund for Development signed a memorandum of understanding that allocated up to $1 billion for sports infrastructure construction in developing countries around the world. But this was not strings-free altruism. The "concessional loans" were a power play, straight-up geopolitics laundered through sport that allowed the Saudis to circulate their surplus capital while appearing to be munificent humanitarians.[171]

The pact followed Donald Trump hosting Saudi Crown Prince Mohammed bin Salman for a glitzy state dinner, where he not only dishonored the memory of journalist Jamal Khashoggi and 9/11 victims—one victim's family member dubbed the gala "a disgusting display"—but also brought together two twenty-first-century sportswashing warlords.[172]

As we've seen, political leaders use sportswashing to deflect attention from entrenched social problems and human-rights violations at home while attempting to appear important on the global stage. But sportswashing doesn't end with reputational repair. It also involves using sports to make political and economic gains. The official state visit spotlights how Trump and MBS are advancing mutually reinforcing strategies of redirection and investment.

The Trump administration organized an enormous, multi-pronged deflective spectacle. At an afternoon presser, when a reporter had the temerity to ask MBS about the US intelligence community's assessment that found the Crown Prince had orchestrated the killing of Khashoggi, Trump intervened, cutting her off mid-sentence. He shrugged off Khashoggi's murder, running interference for the Crown Prince, asserting the journalist was "somebody that was extremely controversial," and adding, "A lot of people didn't like that gentleman that you're talking about. Whether you like him, or didn't like him, things happen." MBS then clumsily broached another hot-button topic: "I feel painful about families of 9/11 in America, but we have to focus on reality."[173] For MBS and Trump, "reality" not only reflects their callous brand of dishonoring the dead. It also means making bank in the name of political dominance.

Behind the shimmering scrim of sportswashing, the privileged sliver of the global 1 percent is free to wheel and deal, pushing their profiteering far beyond the zone of sport. That's where the evening's state dinner comes in. The swanky event featured an array of moneyed creeps and cretins. Apartheid sentimentalist Elon Musk made his ignominious return to the White House. Apple CEO Tim Cook—who has invested more than $2 billion in Saudi Arabian firms in the last five years alone and has vowed to open Apple stores in the country as soon as possible—was on hand. Nvidia's Jensen Huang and Cisco Systems CEO Chuck Robbins—both of whom have sealed deals with the Saudi AI start-up Humain—were there. The list of scheming oligarchs goes on.[174]

The ubiquitous Infantino was also in attendance, bringing his unparalleled obsequiousness to the festivities. The previous week, a low-energy, slurring Trump threatened to move 2026 World Cup matches out of Seattle because of its "liberal-slash-communist mayor," Katie Wilson. He then turned to Infantino for his nod of approval. The FIFA honcho hemmed and hawed, unwilling to defend his own tournament's contract with the city if that meant crossing Trump. He then pivoted, saying that people could expect to "experience a safe and secure World Cup." This seemingly bland stance only gifts additional permission to Trump to ramp up the state security apparatus.[175]

Another conspicuous attendee at the gala dinner was Cristiano Ronaldo, the Portuguese football mega-star whose contract with Al-Nassr of the Saudi Pro League is reportedly worth $700 million. Only the most brain-poisoned soccer fan could miss Ronaldo's craven willingness to put himself at the service of the grotesque trifecta of Trump, Infantino, and MBS. Ronaldo posted a photo of Trump, his wife Georgina Rodríguez, and himself to Instagram, reposted a slow-motion White House video of the couple walking jubilantly with Trump, and snapped a selfie at the state dinner with a gaggle of ghouls, including Infantino, Musk, and Treasury Secretary Howard Lutnick, the latter two Epstein file all-stars.[176] It was Ronaldo's first appearance in the US in nearly a decade, following accusations that first surfaced in 2017 when *Der Spiegel* reported that he raped former schoolteacher Kathryn Mayorga in Las Vegas in 2009, accusations the footballer has denied.[177]

As if to punctuate the fact that Ronaldo was an enthusiastic tool of sportswashing, Trump—who has his own sexual misconduct accusations and convictions—posted on social media that "Ronaldo is a GREAT GUY. Loved meeting him at the White House. Really smart, and cool!!!" along with an AI-generated video of the two playing soccer together.[178] FIFA appeared to agree, magically suspending the red-card penalty Ronaldo received for violent conduct in a World Cup qualifier match against Ireland so that he wouldn't miss a match at the 2026 tournament.[179]

This wasn't the only time Trump has pandered to football stars, choreographing grin-and-grip photo-ops to capitalize on their popularity. In March 2026, he hosted Argentinian mega-star Lionel Messi at the White House to commemorate Inter Miami CF's 2025 MLS Cup victory. Messi is famous for sidestepping sports politics, so the presence of his grinning visage was significant, as was the fact that he was the lone player to enter the room with Trump as "Hail to the Chief" played overhead, while his teammates waited inside on bleachers perched before a slew of cameras. Messi then joined his teammates behind Trump as the president pinballed from political topic to topic for nearly eight fingernails-on-the-chalkboard minutes, rambling on about the war that the United States and Israel were raging on Iran, issuing threats against Cuba, and bragging about the invasion of Venezuela. Messi and his teammates stood there all the while, shuffling from foot to foot, eyes darting about the room.[180] The president blatantly exploited their presence as "the wallpaper for his political and cultural aims," as Pablo Iglesias Maurer wrote in the *Guardian*.[181] Inter Miami played a willing part, presenting Trump with a bright pink Inter Miami jersey emblazoned with "Trump" and "47" as well as an engraved watch and a pink soccer ball bearing Trump's signature. Along the way, Trump took full credit for bringing the World Cup and Olympics to the United States, as if we needed further proof that these events matter deeply to him and his legacy.

This cringe-fest followed Trump's attempts to chum up to players and staff from Juventus FC during the 2025 FIFA Club World Cup. In the painfully awkward White House encounter, Trump blathered on about the possibility of invading Iran, recapitulated his racist travel bans, and pondered whether the US civil war could have been avoided. He also went on an anti-trans rant, putting players on the spot by attempting to elicit their views on transgender women athletes. Trump singled out US internationals on the team—Timothy Weah and Weston McKennie—shaking their hands and pressuring them with a dose of jingoism: "I hope you're going to be the best two players on the field." Weah said afterwards, "It was weird," adding, "I was caught by surprise, honestly, when he started talking politics, with Iran and everything ... They just told us that we have to go, and I had no choice but to go."[182] We can expect more of this—Trump trying to convert the world's best footballers into his own private political pawns—at the 2026 World Cup.

Sportswashing is never just about sports. Behind the grim, blood-stained bacchanal sits an array of massive economic transactions that benefit both bin Salman and Trump.

For MBS, sports create a crucial site not just for image burnishing but also for laundering his country's fossil fuel fortune. While visiting Trump, MBS pledged a whopping $1 trillion in investments in the US. This includes a hefty order for F-35 fighter jets and access to upper-shelf US AI chips.[183] The same week as the state dinner, the Kennedy Center hosted the US-Saudi Investment Forum, a corporate hobnobbing bonanza featuring the likes of Palantir chief executive Alex Karp, Salesforce CEO Marc Benioff, and John Kelly, Global AI's chief technology officer.[184] They mixed and mingled on the red-carpeted interior and clapped for speeches by Trump and MBS. In Trump's remarks, he dubbed the forum a confab of "the world's two leading energy superpowers," who "are partnering on energy like we've never partnered before," thanks to deals cut that week.[185] In separate bilateral talks, Trump referred to the Crown Prince "a very good friend," obscenely noting that "what he's done is incredible in terms of human rights."[186] The reputation-washing has scored swift results, with one 2025 *Los Angeles Times* headline blaring, "Once a Pariah, Saudi Arabia Now Hollywood's Cash Source."[187]

For Trump, Saudi Arabia tees up a massive smash-and-grab for his family. In 2021, soon after Trump departed from his first term in the White House, the Saudi Arabian sovereign wealth fund—overseen by bin Salman—plunged an eye-watering $2 billion into Jared Kushner's company-turned-private equity firm. Meanwhile, Trump's golf courses hosted LIV tournaments, with the Saudi Public Investment Fund covering 100 percent of the costs. The Trump Organization also signed an agreement with a Saudi real-estate firm with plans to build a Trump-branded hotel as one element in a $4 billion elite golf resort in Oman.[188]

In Trump's second term, the grift has only quickened, with a Trump Tower going up in Jeddah, and more real-estate deals with Saudi Arabia on the way.[189] Other countries are registering MBS's lesson. Four days before Trump's

2025 inauguration, the United Arab Emirates royal family invested $500 million in World Financial Liberty, the Trump family's cryptocurrency venture.[190] A *Wall Street Journal* analysis estimated that the Trump family has raked in some $4 billion since the president's reelection.[191] To say that Trump has shredded the Constitution's emoluments clause, which prohibits the president from receiving gifts or payments from foreign powers without congressional consent, would be trafficking in understatement.

The sporting links between the United States and Saudi Arabia smooth the path for this brand of bracing venality, and simultaneously helps desensitize us to the ways that the United States is becoming more like Trump's "very good friends" in Saudi Arabia—the kind of place where a president will scoff at a reporter being cut to pieces with a bone saw right next to the oligarchic thug who ordered the hit.

In March 2025, Dave Zirin and I wrote an essay for *The Nation* titled, "With ICE Out of Control, How Can the US Cohost the 2026 World Cup?" In it, we argued that for the safety of the fans, players, and their families, matches scheduled for the United States needed to be relocated to

Canada and Mexico, and that if FIFA refused to do so, every qualifying country should boycott the World Cup.[192]

It's been done before. The entire continent of Africa boycotted the 1966 World Cup in England. After FIFA allocated only one of sixteen slots at the tournament to Africa—and only if the team could defeat the Asian champion in a playoff match—a rebellion ensued. One Confederation of African Football official described FIFA's egregiously Eurocentric qualification scheme as "a mockery of economics, politics, and geography."[193] As African countries cleaved free from colonialism and gained independence, many leaders viewed football—and specifically the World Cup—as an effective path for advancing their recognition on the global stage. They united in solidarity, and, under the leadership of the pan-Africanist Kwame Nkrumah of Ghana, leveraged football as a space of resistance, refusing to attend the 1966 World Cup. FIFA soon relented, granting automatic qualification berths to both Africa and Asia for the 1970 World Cup in Mexico.[194] The boycott worked.

A few years later, the Soviet Union opted to forgo qualification for the 1974 World Cup, choosing principle over participation. In 1973, after General Augusto Pinochet's coup in Chile, the USSR was slated to play home-and-away playoff matches against Chile for the right to go to the World Cup.

The first match in Moscow was a nil-nil draw. The Soviets then refused to play the second leg in Santiago's *Estadio Nacional* because it had been used as a concentration camp for more than 30,000 supporters of Salvador Allende. FIFA insisted that the match must go on. So, at the kickoff, with no Soviet team on the pitch, Chile kicked off, strolled down the field, and scored into an empty net. Chile qualified for the World Cup in West Germany, while the Soviet Union missed out because of politics.[195]

After Trump returned to office and unleashed mayhem both at home and abroad, calls to boycott the World Cup emerged from Western Europe. German Member of Parliament Jürgen Hardt suggested boycotting the tournament "as a last resort" in order to jar Trump "to his senses." Hardt's parliamentary colleague agreed, adding that he had a "hard time imagining that European countries would take part in the World Cup." Oke Göttlich, a vice-president of the German soccer federation and president of the Bundesliga club St. Pauli—known for its fervent anti-fascist supporters—said it was time to "seriously consider and discuss" a boycott. "The life of a professional player is not worth more than the lives of countless people in various regions who are being directly or indirectly attacked or threatened by the World Cup host," he said. In the UK, more than two dozen politicians from a range of parties put forth a motion demanding "the exclusion of the United States from the World Cup and other major international competitions until it demonstrates clear compliance with international law."[196] A diplomatic boycott is another possibility, as when numerous countries symbolically refused to send diplomats to the 2022 Winter Olympics in Beijing over human-rights abuses in the host country.

While a sporting boycott of the 2026 World Cup is highly unlikely, one thing is certain: campaigners are ramping up to fight the FIFA greed machine. To be sure, disrupting the world's most popular sporting spectacle is no simple matter. The Italian theorist Umberto Eco even argued, "There is one thing that—even if it were essential—no student movement or urban revolt or global protest or what have you would ever be able to do. And that is to occupy the football field." One could "fling Molotov cocktails on the jeeps of any police force" or occupy any religious cathedral, and fewer people would be killed, he wrote, because football inhabits "a deep area of the collective sensibility that no one, whether through conviction or demagogical calculation, will allow to be touched."[197]

Protesting against the World Cup may be complicated, but that hasn't stopped activists who are gearing up in numerous host cities to challenge Trump for "using sports to wash his image," noted Eric Sheehan, an organizer with the anti-Olympics group NOlympicsLA. "We don't think the US deserves to be hosting a global event as it is a perpetrator of war crimes throughout the world and [while ICE is] running a multi-billion-dollar campaign to terrorize residents of host cities and the rest of the United States."[198] This sentiment was echoed by Ajamu Baraka of the Black Alliance for Peace. He told me, "Having the World Cup in the United States at this particular historical moment is not only bizarre, but morally obscene." It risks "normalizing some of the most horrific crimes we have seen committed" in recent US history.[199]

Activists tallied a long list of political reasons why the United States should not be allowed to host, from ICE's reckless pillaging to the invasion of Venezuela to attacks on Iran. Many of them also highlighted that "FIFA is complicit with the aiding and abetting of war crimes and crimes against humanity in Palestine," thereby "facilitating the ongoing Israeli occupation," as LA-based activist Victor Quintero told me. Quintero is an organizer with Peoples Football, a political soccer project in Los Angeles. In late March, Peoples Football organized a soccer festival and political-education event that interspersed 5-a-side soccer with political talks and invitations to get involved in protesting the World Cup. The overall theme was "Football for

Liberation," and numerous community partners showed up in solidarity, such as Stop LAPD Spying, LA Street Care and Mutual Aid, and NOlympicsLA. Sheehan, the organizer with NOlympicsLA, brought along a 3D-printed Jules Rimet replica trophy as a political-education conversation starter. He says he plans on spattering the trophy in fake blood and bringing it to protests ahead of and during the World Cup in Los Angeles. Soccer, writes Stevphen Shukaitis, becomes "not merely a spectacle, but a medium through which new forms of life, solidarity, and resistance might be rehearsed."[200]

FIFA is a classic example of elite capture, which scholar Olúfẹ́mi O. Táíwò describes as a relationship whereby "the advantaged few steer resources and institutions that could serve the many toward their own narrower interests and aims." It's how "socially advantaged people tend to gain control over benefits meant for everyone."[201] When everyday people learn about how FIFA prioritizes profits over people, it makes an impression—and not a good one. Infantino, Trump, bin Salman, and their collaborators have the upper hand, but will they have the last word?

Conclusion: A Blast from the Future

There is no way that the United States should be hosting the 2026 World Cup. Under President Donald Trump, the United States is an openly rogue regime: barbarism in a blue suit backed by khaki camo. Masked ICE thugs are marauding throughout the country, kidnapping everyday people—including US citizens—without legitimate cause. This is not a safe place to visit to watch football. Those who absolutely must attend the World Cup should do so in Mexico and Canada. The United States has come off its hinges.

Trump does not deserve the chance to suck the joy out of the world's game, to use it as an opportunity to sportswash, deflecting attention from his toxic havoc at home and abroad, while teeing himself up for political gain and personal enrichment. Sportswashing is an ethical morass that corrupts sport's most cherished values of community, camaraderie, and belonging, while co-opting fans into agonizing complicity—largely against their will.[202]

FIFA claims to be both a beacon of human rights and its devoted safeguard. The group's own guiding statutes unequivocally proclaim that "FIFA is committed to respecting all internationally recognized human rights and shall strive to promote the protection of these rights."[203] And a key goal of FIFA President Gianni Infantino's "Strategic Objectives for the Global Game: 2023-2027" claims to value his organization's responsibility for upholding human rights.[204] Back in 2017, the United 2026 bid vowed that each host city would issue a human-rights plan by August 2025, but that deadline passed without a single US city complying. The patchwork of human-rights plans that eventually emerged has lacked both meaningful opportunities for public input and toothless enforcement mechanisms.[205] Meanwhile, the United States has—in broad daylight for all to see—become a human-rights-violating machine under Trump. Infantino has not only remained silent; he has fluffed Trump's ego at every turn. Their shared passion for rapacious financial extraction supersedes any baseline sense of morality, let alone respect for human rights.

FIFA's defenders often point to the need for neutrality in a politically polarized world. After all, FIFA's statutes demand that it "remains neutral in matters of politics and religion."[206]

FIFA's "Code of Ethics" even includes a "code of neutrality" when it comes to "dealings with government institutions, national and international organizations." Violators face a potential ban from the sport of up to two years.[207] But the reality is that FIFA's neutrality stance is a cagey form of bias that forever slants in favor of those in power. FIFA-style neutrality is a mere alibi for maintaining the status quo, and it has ramifications far beyond the 2026 World Cup.

To see FIFA's problematic brand of neutrality in action, look no further than its treatment of Israel and Palestine, both of which are FIFA member states. When Russia invaded Ukraine in 2022, FIFA moved with lightning speed, barring Russia from all competitions only four days later. And yet, when it comes to Israel, FIFA has foot-dragged, even though the country appears to be blatantly violating FIFA rules regarding human rights. The organization's statutes state unambiguously that "Member associations and their clubs may not play on the territory of another member association without the latter's approval."[208] And yet, according to Human Rights Watch, the Israel Football Association has long been staging soccer matches on "settlements in the West Bank on land unlawfully taken from Palestinians." The United Nations has identified at least eight Israeli soccer clubs that have either developed or played matches "in Israeli colonial settlements of the occupied West Bank." In addition, many clubs in the Israel Football Association "have exhibited racism towards the Palestinian people and players over the years," a clear violation of FIFA's non-discrimination policies. But FIFA has slow-rolled the Palestinian Football Association's efforts to achieve justice on these issues through the world governing body for soccer's internal channels.[209]

In late March 2026, FIFA finally issued its rulings. In one, FIFA's Governance, Audit, and Compliance Committee quite remarkably decided that no action was required because "the final legal status of the West Bank remains an unresolved and highly complex matter under public international law," even though this contradicted the International Criminal Court and the informed opinion of a cavalcade of human-rights specialists. In a separate ruling, FIFA's Disciplinary Committee found that the Israel Football Association (IFA) failed to properly curtail racist behavior by the Israeli soccer club Beitar Jerusalem FC. Its penalty? A trifling fine, a "warning," and a requirement "to display in its next three A-level FIFA competition matches at home a significant and highly visible banner with the words 'Football United the World—No to Discrimination' alongside the Israeli Football Association's logo." That's it. Such selective impunity cuts an even wider path for authoritarianism.[210]

More than any leader in sport, Infantino has enabled the global swerve toward fascism. To toady up to Trump, he even moved residence to Miami—around 70 miles down the road from Mar-a-Lago—where FIFA reportedly foots the $5,000-per-month bill for his daughter to attend private school.[211] Infantino's presence at the inaugural "Board of Peace" meeting was a dangerous farce. In his remarks, he offered cut-and-paste pablum about FIFA "uniting the world." To emphasize the point, he turned to Trump and said, "Mr. President, we will unite the world here this summer during the World Cup." FIFA's post-event press release heralded "a landmark partnership agreement" that "aims to provide a comprehensive recovery program for Gaza." Who would direct such an enterprise? The agreement was signed by "Gaza Executive Board of Peace member Yakir Gabay," who, from his title, one might surmise hails from the Palestinian territories.[212] Nope. Gabay is an Israeli billionaire real-estate magnate who resides in Cyprus.[213] FIFA is a brazen accomplice to what increasingly looks like a repeat of the 1948 mass expulsion of Palestinians: a Nakba 2.0.

FIFA is unreformable from within. The human-rights group FairSquare gets it exactly right when it asserts, "Football's ruling institutions...can no longer be allowed to claim that they and the game are autonomous when they are so obviously beholden to the economically and politically powerful. They can no longer be allowed to exist in a legal gray area where there is no oversight, no limits on how power is wielded, no space to challenge and contest its rules and the decisions of its rulers."[214] Even after the epic corruption scandal of 2015, FIFA wriggled free from instituting meaningful reforms. Their tactic is to be so constantly changing that they never really have to change at all.

FIFA's patron-client relations are stronger than ever. "Because its senior officials and a critical mass of its member associations are locked into a mutually dependent system of patronage," writes FairSquare, "only external regulation can impose the model of governance that will provide the foundations for FIFA to deliver on football's potential and to prevent the organization from causing more serious harm."[215] I agree, but would go even further. FIFA must be scrapped and rebuilt from the ground up.

Trump follows a long line of autocrats who understood the power of associating themselves with famous athletes and athleticism. Embracing sport has long been a go-to move in the authoritarian playbook, as we saw with Mussolini and the 1934 World Cup, the Argentinian generals in 1978, and Putin in the twenty-first century. An extension of this dynamic is the calculated self-presentation of authoritarians engaged in sports themselves. This taps into the dimension of authoritarianism rooted in paternalistic machismo. Autocrats as diverse as North Korea's Kim Jong Il, Sheikh Zayed of the United Arab Emirates, and Uganda's Idi Amin issued propaganda touting their sporting prowess, in golf, falconry, and boxing, respectively.[216] Putin, of course, has his judo, hockey, and bare-chested horse-riding. Trump has added his own tacky twist on this tradition. He has golfed one out of every four days in office (and in doing so, is on track to rack up some $300 million in secret-service costs in his second term alone).[217]

Sports are a key component of the Trump brand. As we have seen, the Trump regime is using sports to help shepherd in a USAmerican variant of the "new model of state-oligarchic capitalism" advanced by previous autocrats. In doing so, he's piling up the pathetic machismo sky-high. Amid the World Cup hubbub, Trump has planned a UFC event on the White House lawn to celebrate the country's 250th birthday. Journalist Karim Zidan described it as "authoritarian theater," and "a stage for MAGA mythology" that "carries shades of fascist Italy under Benito Mussolini, particularly its obsession with masculinity, spectacle, and nationalism."[218] In announcing Markwayne Mullin to replace the disgraced Homeland Security Secretary Kristi Noem, Trump emphasized the Oklahoma Senator's sporting credentials as a "former undefeated professional MMA fighter."[219]

Sportswashing is not going away anytime soon. With sports mega-events on the horizon such as the Los Angeles 2028 Summer Olympics—which are slated to be held toward the end of Trump's second term—as well as the 2034 Saudi Arabia World Cup and the possibility of a 2036 Olympics in India under Narendra Modi, this is an idea with a future.[220] After all, FIFA is not the only global sports body with a stated preference for autocrats. The late International Olympic Committee member Gian-Franco Kasper admitted, in a moment of stark candor in 2019, that authoritarians brought real perks to the Olympics. "Dictators can perhaps carry out such events," he said. "They do not have to ask the people."[221]

If "the people" and their representatives in Los Angeles were asked whether they wanted Casey Wasserman to continue to lead the 2028 Olympics, many of them, including Mayor Karen Bass and a sizable chunk of the City Council, would say hell no. Wasserman, the well-connected sports and music mogul and grandson of Hollywood powerbroker Lew Wasserman, came under fire when he appeared in the Epstein files, engaging in disturbing email correspondence with Ghislaine Maxwell.[222] But that is not the only moral obscenity that stains his record. When ICE rampaged through Los Angeles—and when Trump even sent in the military—LA28, unlike other sports organizations in the city, sat utterly silent. Before that, when Trump went on an anti-trans rant at a press conference marking the creation of the 2028 Los Angeles Olympics Task Force in August 2025, Wasserman was among the first to clap in approval. When tyrants like Trump see this sort of weak-kneed obsequiousness, they lick their lips.

Paradoxically, the weaker Trump gets, the more dangerous he becomes. The lower his approval ratings sink, the more he leans on the power of sport to pump up his popularity. However, there is no guarantee that this strategy will work. Sportswashing—and all the media attention it brings—opens up possibilities for pushback, exposing cracks in the shimmering spectacle of power that can be exploited by savvy activists and people of principle. Recognition of sportswashing's power is the first step toward its resistance.

Soccer brings us joy. It gifts us with fellowship, camaraderie, community, and fun. In its best moments, football can create a world full of wonder that sidesteps, if momentarily, capitalism's tendency toward premature foreclosure. Soccer has brought me enormous personal joy and satisfaction over the years, from joining my first team as a four-year-old to playing for the US U-23 men's national team in international competition to enjoying a professional career. Football can be transformative. It is powerful. But that power arrives with responsibility, and FIFA, as overseer of the global game, has failed in its responsibility, dulling football's rich palette and replacing it with a capitalist hellscape.

But the battle is far from done. "I think the grassroots are really the stewards of the game, and FIFA is the cancer of the game," said Victor Quintero, the organizer with Peoples Football in Los Angeles. "It's up to working-class people to revive the spirit of what football is." For Quintero, football means fightback. "Peoples Football uses football as a site of struggle. Because it's such an international sport, it gives us an opportunity to agitate and to highlight the contradictions."[223]

So, the 2026 World Cup gives us an opportunity to say no, but also to say yes. We're living a pick-a-side moment in history when one must choose democracy or authoritarianism. If someone refuses to choose, then in reality, they have chosen. To that battle, I say, game on.

Notes

1 FIFA, "FIFA Introduces the FIFA Peace Prize – An Award to Recognise Exceptional Actions for Peace and Unity," November 5, 2025, https://inside.fifa.com/organisation/media-releases/peace-prize-award-football-unites-the-world-infantino?requester=MediaHub

2 Dave Zirin and Jules Boykoff, "FIFA Kisses Up to Trump With a 'Peace Prize'," *The Nation*, December 5, 2025, https://www.thenation.com/article/society/fifa-trump-infantino-peace-prize/

3 Bryan Armen Graham, "Trump Loomed Over Sport Like Never Before in 2025. Next Year He Will Take Even More, *Guardian*, December 24, 2025, https://www.theguardian.com/sport/2025/dec/24/donald-trump-sports-world-cup-ufc-white-house

4 Matt Slater, "FIFA Opens New York Office in U.S. President's Trump Tower," *New York Times*, July 8, 2025, https://www.nytimes.com/athletic/6479639/2025/07/08/fifa-trump-tower-new-york-club-world-cup/

5 Jules Boykoff, "Toward a Theory of Sportswashing: Mega-Events, Soft Power, and Political Conflict," *Sociology of Sport Journal*, Vol. 39, No. 4 (2022): 342-351.

6 Roger Best and Dennis Howard, *The Business of Sports: Fan Engagement, Sports Products, and Sports Participation*, 2nd edition (Eugene, OR: Global Sports Insights, LLC, 2023), 14.

7 Dorie Chevlen and Ronda Kaysen, "LA Rams Owner Stan Kroenke Becomes Largest Private Landowner in the US," *New York Times*, January 25, 2026, 9.

8 RickCole,'TheGlobalBrand:AnAppreciationoftheOlympic Rings', *Smith Communication Partners*, 21 July 2021; Barnaby Lane, "2026 World Cup: The Most-Watched Sporting Event in History?" *Sports Illustrated*, December 3, 2025, https://www.si.com/soccer/2026-world-cup-the-most-watched-sporting-event-history

9 Dmitry Braginsky, "Dmitry Shostakovich, Sport and Politics in the USSR," *Sport in Society*, Vol. 17, No. 3 (2014): 345-357.

10 Umberto Eco, "Sports Chatter," in *Faith in Fakes: Essays*, Trans. William Weaver (London: Secker & Warburg: 1986), 160.

11 Quoted in Eduardo Galeano, *Soccer in Sun and Shadow*, Trans. Mark Fried (New York: *Nation Books*, 2013), 37.

12 Camille Robcis, "Frantz Fanon, Institutional Psychotherapy, and the Decolonization of Psychiatry," *Journal of the History of Ideas* Vol. 81, Number 2 (2020): 303-325.

13 Zirin and Jules Boykoff, "FIFA Kisses Up to Trump With a 'Peace Prize.'"

14 Galeano, *Soccer in Sun and Shadow*, 12.

15 Dennis Young, "All the Sports Figures Attending Trump's Second Inauguration," *Front Office Sports*, January 20,

2026, https://frontofficesports.com/athletes-owners-executives-trump-inauguration-updates/

16 Dan Sheldon, "IOC Clears FIFA President Gianni Infantino of Breaching Political Neutrality Rules," *New York Times,* February 22, 2026, https://www.nytimes.com/athletic/7063316/2026/02/22/gianni-infantino-fifa-ioc-trump-political-neutrality/

17 Adam Crafton, "Gianni Infantino Claims FIFA Received More Than One Million Ticket Requests for 77 World Cup Games," *New York Times,* February 19, 2026, https://www.nytimes.com/athletic/7058071/2026/02/19/gianni-infantino-fifa-world-cup-games-tickets/

18 Jules Boykoff, "Donald Trump's Return to Power Lays Bare the Lie that Sports Don't Matter," *Guardian,* January 21, 2025, https://www.theguardian.com/sport/2025/jan/21/trump-sports-politics-democrats

19 White House, "Keeping Men Out of Women's Sports," February 5, 2025, https://www.whitehouse.gov/presidential-actions/2025/02/keeping-men-out-of-womens-sports/; White House, "Saving College Sports," July 24, 2025, https://www.whitehouse.gov/presidential-actions/2025/07/saving-college-sports/

20 "Trump Booed at Commanders NFL Game Before Calling PlaysfromFoxBroadcastBooth,*Guardian,*November9,2025, https://www.theguardian.com/sport/2025/nov/09/donald-trump-commanders-nfl-game-fan-reaction

21 Brett Okamoto, "Dana White on UFC's White House Card: 'We Got It Done'," *ESPN,* August 28, 2025, https://www.espn.com/mma/story/_/id/46100519/dana-white-ufc-white-house-card-got-done

22 Cathal Kelly, "Donald Trump Isn't Athletic, But He's the Sportsperson of the Year," *The Globe and Mail*, December 26, 2025, https://www.theglobeandmail.com/sports/article-donald-trump-sportsperson-of-the-year/

23 Dave Zirin and Jules Boykoff, "The Ugly Underbelly of the US Men's Hockey Victory," *The Nation*, February 23, 2026, https://www.thenation.com/article/society/us-hockey-olympics-gold-trump/; "Full Transcript of Trump's State of the Union Address," *New York Times*, February 25, 2026, https://www.nytimes.com/2026/02/25/us/politics/state-of-the-union-transcript-trump.html

24 Karim Zidan, "The Network Behind Trump's Sporting Power," *Play the Game*, nd, https://www.playthegame.org/projects/trump-and-sport/the-network-behind-trump-s-sporting-power/

25 The American Presidency Project, "Remarks Announcing the 2026 Federation Internationale de Football Association (FIFA) World Cup Draw Location and an Exchange with Reporters," UC Santa Barbara, August 22, 2025, https://www.presidency.ucsb.edu/documents/remarks-announcing-the-2026-federation-internationale-de-football-association-fifa-world

26 "Less Democracy Makes for an Easier World Cup," *Reuters*, April 24, 2014, http://uk.reuters.com/article/2013/04/24/uk-soccer-fifa-idUKBRE93N17F20130424

27 Chris Walker, "After Davos Speech, Trump Tells the World, 'Sometimes, You Need a Dictator'," *Truthout*, January 22, 2026, https://truthout.org/articles/after-davos-speech-trump-tells-the-world-sometimes-you-need-a-dictator/

28 Steven Levitsky, Lucan A. Way, and Daniel Ziblatt, "The Price of American Authoritarianism: What Can Reverse Democratic Decline?" *Foreign Affairs*, Vol. 105, Number 1 (2026): 30-43. 30-31.

29 Levitsky, Way, and Ziblatt, "The Price of American Authoritarianism," 33.

30 Matthew Purdy, "Trump Remakes America as Leader of the Brand," *New York Times*, December 27, 2025, https://www.nytimes.com/2025/12/27/us/politics/trump-renaming.html; Michael Gold, "Officials Pressed Schumer to Help Name Penn Station and Dulles Airport for Trump," *New York Times*, February 6, 2026, https://www.nytimes.com/2026/02/06/us/politics/trump-schumer-penn-station-dulles-airport-renaming.html

31 United States Secret Service, "2028 Olympic and Paralympic Games in Los Angeles Designated a National Special Security Event," June 13, 2024, https://www.secretservice.gov/newsroom/releases/2024/06/2028-olympic-and-paralympic-games-los-angeles-designated-national-special

32 Joseph Nye, *Soft Power: The Means to Succeed in World Politics* (New York: Public Affairs, 2004), 5.

33 Morgan Campbell, "Sports Worship Winners, But Donald Trump Is Recent History's Sorest Loser," *CBC*, January 13, 2021, https://www.cbc.ca/sports/opinion-donald-trump-sports-industry-1.5870838

34 Donald Trump with Tony Schwartz, *Trump: The Art of the Deal* (New York: Random House, 1987), 181.

35 The American Presidency Project, "Remarks Announcing…"

36 Gulnara Akhundova, "Baku European Games 2015: A Fearsome PR Machine is Using Sport to Sweep Human Rights Under the Carpet," *The Independent,* June 12, 2015. https://www.independent.co.uk/voices/comment/baku-european-games-2015-a-fearsome-pr-machine-is-using-sport-to-sweep-human-rights-under-the-carpet-10314316.html; Rebecca Vincent and Sport for Rights, 2015. *Sport for rights European games press briefing.* https://static.poder360.com.br/2021/10/Sport-for-rights-Eurpean-Games-2015-Release.pdf

37 Harriet Sherwood, "'Sums up 2022': Permacrisis Chosen as Collins Word of the Year," *Guardian,* November 1, 2022, https://www.theguardian.com/culture/2022/nov/01/sums-up-2022-permacrisis-chosen-as-collins-word-of-the-year

38 Boykoff, "Toward a Theory of Sportswashing."

39 Braginsky, "Dmitry Shostakovich, Sport and Politics in the USSR," 346, 355.

40 David Yallop, *How They Stole the Game* (London: Constable, 2011), 23.

41 Alan Tomlinson, *What Is FIFA For?* (Bristol: Bristol University Press, 2026), 22.

42 David Goldblatt, *The Ball Is Round: A Global History of Soccer* (New York: Riverhead Books, 2006), 230.

43 Lorenzo Jalabert D'Amado, "Montevideo 1930: Reassessing the Selection of the First World Cup Host," *Soccer & Society,* Vol. 21, No. 8 (2020): 848-860. 850.

44 Arnaldo Cortesi, "All Italy Focused on Football Game," *New York Times,* March 25, 1928, 164.

45 Nicola Sbetti and Daniele Serapiglia, "Was Football Fascist?: The 1934 World Cup in the Postwar Memory," *Soccer & Society*, Vol. 21, No. 8 (2020): 889-903.
46 Jonathan Wilson, *The Power and the Glory: The History of the World Cup* (New York: Bold Type Books, 2025), 44-45.
47 Goldblatt, *The Ball Is Round*, 259.
48 Wilson, *The Power and the Glory*, 53.
49 Quoted in Goldblatt, *The Ball Is Round*, 254.
50 Avery Brundage, "Brundage Hails Spread of Sports on Large Scale in Other Nations," *New York Times*, January 12, 1935, 19.
51 Jules Boykoff, *The 1936 Berlin Olympics: Race, Power, and Sportswashing* (Common Ground Publishing, 2023), Chapter 2.
52 Boykoff, *The 1936 Berlin Olympics*, Chapter 4.
53 Frederick T. Birchall, "100,000 Hail Hitler; US Athletes Avoid Nazi Salute to Him," *New York Times*, August 2, 1936, 1.
54 Frederick T. Birchall, "Olympics Leave Glow of Pride in the Reich," *New York Times*, August 16, 1936, E5.
55 Oliver Hilmes, *Berlin 1936: Sixteen Days in August*, Trans. Jefferson Chase. (New York: Other Press, 2018), 98.
56 Boykoff, *The 1936 Berlin Olympics*, Epilogue.
57 National Security Archives, "Inside Argentina's Killing Machine: U.S. Intelligence Documents Record Gruesome Human Rights Crimes of 1976-1983," May 30, 2019, https://nsarchive.gwu.edu/briefing-book/southern-cone/2019-05-30/inside-argentinas-killing-machine-us-intelligence-documents-record-gruesome-human-rights-crimes-1976

58 Yallop, *How They Stole the Game,* 184-186.
59 Nicolás Sagaian, "Videla's Guest of Honour." Papelitos, 2018, http://papelitos.com.ar/nota/henry-kissinger-en-el-mundial-78
60 Grant Farred, *Long Distance Love: A Passion for Football* (Philadelphia: Temple University Press, 2008), 62.
61 Lívia Gonçalves Magalhães, "40 Years After Victory: Disputing Memories over the 1978 World Cup in Argentina," *Soccer & Society,* Vol. 21, No. 8 (2020): 904-917. 906.
62 Bill L. Smith, "The Argentinian Junta and the Press," *Soccer & Society,* Vol. 3, Number 1 (2002): 69-78. 75.
63 Adam Scharpf, Christian Gläßel, and Pearce Edwards, "International Sports Events and Repression in Autocracies: Evidence from the 1978 FIFA World Cup," *American Political Science Review,* Vol. 117, Issue 3, (2023): 909–926.
64 Simon Kuper, *Soccer Against the Enemy: How the World's Most Popular Sport Starts and Fuels Revolutions and Keeps Dictators in Power* (New York: Nation Books, 2006), 212, 215.
65 David Winner, "Dangerous Games," *Financial Times,* June 20, 2008, https://www.ft.com/content/98507370-3c0e-11dd-9cb2-0000779fd2ac
66 Quoted in Wilson, *The Power and the Glory,* 360.
67 Quoted in Goldblatt, *The Ball Is Round,* 523.
68 Yallop, *How They Stole the Game,* 128-129.
69 Alan Tomlinson, "The Supreme Leader Sails On: Leadership, Ethics and Governance in FIFA," *Sport in Society,* Vol. 17, Number 9 (2014): 1155-1169. 1159.

70 Alan Tomlinson, *FIFA: The Men, the Myths, the Money* (London and New York: Routledge, 2014), 23.
71 Cindy Boren, "Ex-FIFA Official Had $6,000-a-month Trump Tower Apartment for Unruly Cats," *Washington Post*, May 27, 2015, https://www.washingtonpost.com/news/early-lead/wp/2015/05/27/ex-fifa-official-had-6000-a-month-trump-tower-apartment-for-unruly-cats/
72 Ken Bensinger, *Red Card: How the U.S. Blew the Whistle on the World's Biggest Sports Scandal* (New York: Simon & Schuster, 2018); David Conn, *The Fall of the House of FIFA: The Multimillion-Dollar Corruption at the Heart of Global Soccer* (New York: Nation Books, 2017).
73 Pankaj Mishra, *Age of Anger: A History of the Present* (New York: Picador, 2017), 81.
74 Michael J. Garcia and Cornel Borbély, "Report on the Inquiry into the 2018/2022 FIFA World Cup™ Bidding Process," September 2014, 1-353. 331.
75 Andrew Keh, "In Long-Secret FIFA Report, More Details but No Smoking Gun," *New York Times*, June 28, 2017, B8.
76 FairSquare, "Joint Statement on FIFA Misgovernance," May 27, 2025, https://fairsq.org/wp-content/uploads/2025/05/FIFA-Reforms-Statement-2025.pdf
77 US Mission Uzbekistan, "U.S. Special Envoy for Global Partnerships Paolo Zampolli Returns to Uzbekistan for Olympic Council of Asia General Assembly," January 23, 2026, https://uz.usembassy.gov/u-s-special-envoy-for-global-partnerships-paolo-zampolli-returns-to-uzbekistan-for-olympic-council-of-asia-general-assembly/
78 Sven Daniel Wolfe "'For the Benefit of Our Nation': Unstable Soft Power in the 2018 Men's World Cup in

Russia." *International Journal of Sport Policy and Politics,* Vol. 12, Issue 4 (2020): 545-561. 552.

79 Wolfe, "'For the Benefit of Our Nation'," 553.

80 Wolfe, "'For the Benefit of Our Nation'," 555.

81 Anna Alekseyeva, "Sochi 2014 and the Rhetoric of a New Russia: Image Construction through Mega-events," *East European Politics,* Vol. 30, Number 2 (2014): 158-174.

82 Jonathan Grix and Ninà Kramareva, "The Sochi Winter Olympics and Russia's Unique Soft Power Strategy" *Sport in Society,* Vol. 20, Number 4 (2017): 461-475.

83 Human Rights Watch, "Russia's Worst Crackdown Since Soviet Era," January 31, 2023, https://www.hrw.org/news/2013/01/31/russia-worst-crackdown-soviet-era

84 Human Rights Watch, "Human Rights Guide for Reporters: 2018 FIFA World Cup in Russia," 2018, 1-44, https://www.hrw.org/sites/default/files/news_attachments/reporters_guide_world_cup0518_pdfweb_0.pdf

85 "Watch as Vladimir Putin Plays Football with FIFA's Gianni Infantino," *Sky Sports,* March 6, 2018, https://www.skysports.com/football/news/13956/11278447/watchStatutes-as-vladimir-putin-plays-football-with-fifas-gianni-infantino

86 Shaun Walker, "Russians Protest Over Pension Age Rise Announced During World Cup," *Guardian,* July 1, 2018, https://www.theguardian.com/world/2018/jul/01/russians-protest-pension-age-rise-announced-during-world-cup

87 Andrew Tan-Delli Cicchi and Dave Zirin, "FIFA's Weak Attempts to Fight Racism Are on Display at the World Cup in Russia," *The Nation,* June 20, 2018, https://www.

thenation.com/article/archive/fifas-weak-attempts-fight-racism-display-world-cup-russia/

88 FairSquare, "Substitute: The Case for External Reform for FIFA," October 2024, 1-174; Tariq Panja, "The World Cup's Hot New Accessory Comes with a Few Questions," *New York Times,* July 3, 2018, https://www.nytimes.com/2018/07/03/sports/world-cup/fan-id-badges.html

89 Peter Rutland, "Putin's Economic Record: Is the Oil Boom Sustainable?" in *Power and Policy in Putin's Russia,* ed. Richard Sakwa (London and New York: Routledge, 2009), 173-194. 181, 179.

90 Jules Boykoff, "Celebration Capitalism and the Sochi 2014 Winter Olympics," *Olympika: The International Journal of Olympic Studies* Vol. 22 (2013): 39-70.

91 Sven Daniel Wolfe and Martin Müller, "Crisis Neopatrimonialism," *Problems of Post-Communism,* Vol. 65, Number 2 (2018): 101-114. 102, 105.

92 Shaun Walker, "Russians Protest Over Pension Age Rise Announced During World Cup," *Guardian,* July 1, 2018, https://www.theguardian.com/world/2018/jul/01/russians-protest-pension-age-rise-announced-during-world-cup

93 FairSquare, "Substitute."

94 AmieFerris-Rotman, "'Let Us Be Free;: Iranian Women Mount Protest Over Stadium Ban at World Cup Match," *Washington Post,* June 15, 2018, https://www.washingtonpost.com/world/europe/let-us-be-free-iranian-women-mount-protest-over-stadium-ban-at-world-cup-match/2018/06/15/9755dd1e-6fdb-11e8-b4d8-eaf78d4c544c_story.html

95 Olesya Gerasimenko, "Russia World Cup: How Pussy Riot Managed to Burst into Final," *BBC*, July 20, 2018, https://www.bbc.com/news/world-europe-44886550

96 "Putin Honours FIFA's Infantino with State Medal Over 2018 World Cup, *Reuters*, May 21, 2019, https://www.reuters.com/article/sports/-putin-honours-fifas-infantino-with-state-medal-over-2018-world-cup-idUSKCN1ST1LF/

97 Vitaly Kazakov and Dmitrijs Andrejevs, "The Eastern European Mega-Event Decade: Sports, Geopolitics, and War at the Start of the Twenty-First Century," in Sven Daniel Wolfe, ed. *The Hard Edge of Soft Power: Mega-Events, Geopolitics, and Making Nations Great Again* (Singapore: Palgrave Macmillan, 2025), 113-127. 121

98 Associated Press, "Today I Feel Gay, I Feel Disabled, I Feel a Migrant Worker," November 19, 2022, https://www.youtube.com/watch?v=oP3e5IV-Thw

99 Associated Press, "Today I Feel Gay, I Feel Disabled, I Feel a Migrant Worker," November 19, 2022, https://www.youtube.com/watch?v=oP3e5IV-Thw Along the way, Infantino made half of a decent point, calling out Western hypocrisy: "I think for what we Europeans have been doing in the last 3,000 years around the world we should be apologizing for [the] next 3,000 years before starting to give moral lessons to people."

100 Human Rights Watch, "Red Card: Exploitation of Construction Workers on World Cup Sites in Russia," June 14, 2017, https://www.hrw.org/report/2017/06/14/redcard/exploitation-of-construction-workers-on-world-cup-sites-in-russia

101 Håvard Melnæs, "The Slaves of St Petersburg" *Josimar*, March 28, 2017, https://josimarfootball.com/2017/03/28/the-slaves-of-st-petersburg/

102 Pete Pattisson, et al., "Revealed: 6,500 migrant workers have died in Qatar since World Cup awarded," *The Guardian*, February 23, 2021, https://www.theguardian.com/global-development/2021/feb/23/revealed-migrant-worker-deaths-qatar-fifa-world-cup-2022; Human Rights Watch, "FIFA: Pay for Qatar's Migrant Workers," May 18, 2022, https://www.hrw.org/news/2022/05/18/fifa-pay-harm-qatars-migrant-workers

103 Paul MacInnis, "FIFA Ignores Own Report into Qatar World Cup Over Workers' Compensation," *Guardian*, November 30, 2024, https://www.theguardian.com/football/2024/nov/30/fifa-ignores-own-report-into-qatar-world-cup-over-workers-compensation

104 Karim Zidan, "Whistleblower Reveals Qatar's Surveillance of Journalists During 2022 World Cup Preparations," *Play the Game*, October 8, 2025, https://www.playthegame.org/news/abdullah-ibhais-reveals-qatar-s-surveillance-of-journalists-during-2022-world-cup-preparations/

105 Rémi Dupré, "2022 World Cup: The Close Ties Between Qatar and FIFA President Gianni Infantino," *Le Monde*, November 19, 2022, https://www.lemonde.fr/en/football/article/2022/11/19/2022-world-cup-the-close-ties-between-qatar-and-fifa-president-gianni-infantino_6004906_130.html

106 Sarath Ganji, "How Qatar Became a World Leader in Sportswashing," *Journal of Democracy*, November

2022, https://www.journalofdemocracy.org/how-qatar-became-a-world-leader-in-sportswashing/; Paul Michael Brannagan and Richard Giulianotti, "Soft Power and Soft Disempowerment: Qatar, Global Sport and Football's 2022 World Cup Finals," *Leisure Studies*, Vol. 34, Issue 6 (2015): 703-719.

107 Jules Boykoff, "The World Cup in Qatar Is a Climate Catastrophe," *Scientific American*, November 23, 2022, https://www.scientificamerican.com/article/the-world-cup-in-qatar-is-a-climate-catastrophe/

108 Human Rights Watch, "Qatar: Significant Labor and Kafala Reforms," September 24, 2020, https://www.hrw.org/news/2020/09/24/qatar-significant-labor-and-kafala-reforms

109 Dave Zirin and Jules Boykoff, "Palestine: The Unexpected Star of the 2022 World Cup," *The Nation*, December 7, 2022, https://www.thenation.com/article/world/palestine-world-cup-2022/

110 Noenoe K. Silva, *Aloha Betrayed: Native Hawaiian Resistance to American Colonialism* (Durham and London, UK: Duke University Press, 2004), 163.

111 "Text of the Letter from O.J. Simpson," *New York Times*, June 17, 1994, 10.

112 Tony Mason, *Passion of the People?: Football in South America* (London and New York, Verso, 1995), 134.

113 Yallop, *How They Stole the Game*, 275-277.

114 Mason, *Passion of the People?*, 152.

115 Robert A. Baade and Victor Matheson, "The Quest for the Cup: Assessing the Economic Impact of the World Cup,"

Regional Studies, Vol. 38, No. 4 (2004): 343-354. 351, emphasis added.

116 Yallop, *How They Stole the Games,* 275.

117 Neil deMause, "If MLS Isn't a Ponzi Scheme, Maybe It's the WeWork of Sports?" *Field of Schemes,* November 5, 2019, https://www.fieldofschemes.com/2019/11/05/15426/if-mls-isnt-a-ponzi-scheme-maybe-its-the-wework-of-sports/, emphasis in original

118 Henry Bushnell et al, "100 World Cup 2026 Questions Answered," *New York Times,* March 3, 2026, https://www.nytimes.com/athletic/7059445/2026/03/03/world-cup-questions-soccer-beginner-explained/

119 United 2026 Bid Book, "Unity. Certainty. Opportunity." 2017, Introduction, https://digitalhub.fifa.com/m/3c077448dcd5c0ab/original/w3yjeu7dadt5erw26wmu-pdf.pdf

120 The American Presidency Project, "Remarks Announcing…"

121 United 2026 Bid Book, "Unity. Certainty. Opportunity." 455.

122 Human Rights Watch, "World Cup 2026: FIFA Needs to Act on Human Rights," December 3, 2025, https://www.hrw.org/news/2025/12/03/world-cup-2026-fifa-needs-to-act-on-human-rights

123 Andrew Das, "How 3 Letters From Trump Might Help Bring the 2026 World Cup to the US," *New York Times,* June 12, 2018, https://www.nytimes.com/2018/06/12/sports/trump-letters-world-cup.html

124 Ghonech Habibiazad and Robert Greenall, "At Least 153 Dead After Reported Strike on School, Iran Says," *BBC,* March 1, 2026, https://www.bbc.com/news/articles/

c1l7rvqq51eo; Mahmoud Aslan, "After a Sports Hall in Iran Was Bombed, Witnesses Describe Chaos and 'Continuous Screaming,'" *Drop Site,* March 1, 2026, https://www.dropsitenews.com/p/iran-lamerd-sports-hall-teenage-girls-killed-us-israel-war

125 "Donald Trump 'Really Does Not Care' If Iran Play at World Cup 2026," *Guardian,* March 4, 2026, https://www.theguardian.com/football/2026/mar/04/donald-trump-really-does-not-care-if-iran-play-at-football-world-cup-2026

126 Matt Hughes, "Iran's Sports Minister Says Football Team Will Not Play at 2026 World Cup," *Guardian,* March 11, 2026, https://www.theguardian.com/football/2026/mar/11/donald-trumpcode language-iran-welcome-2026-world-cup-gianni-infantino

127 Donald J. Trump, Truth Social, March 12, 2026, https://truthsocial.com/@realDonaldTrump/posts/116216801278101254

128 FairSquare, "Substitute," 106.

129 FIFA, "Bid Evaluation Report: 2026 FIFA World Cup™," 2018, 1-224, https://digitalhub.fifa.com/m/55d1d154bdd6324/original/ir3g14juxglqbbteevvf-pdf.pdf

130 FIFA, "Overview of Government Guarantees and the Government Declaration," nd, 1-12, https://digitalhub.fifa.com/m/502252882e0edd0e/original/ufybnq0f1kd2g1n-hw5pc-pdf.pdf

131 Personal interview with Nick McGeehan, November 4, 2025.

132 Sophia Cai, "US Cities Confront FIFA Over World Cup Costs," August 31, 2025, https://www.politico.com/news/2025/08/31/world-cup-us-host-city-cost-00528429

133 Tomlinson, *What Is FIFA For?*, 67; FIFA, "Revised Budget 2023-2026," nd, https://inside.fifa.com/official-documents/annual-report/2024/financials/revised-2023-2026-budget

134 FIFA, "Partners," nd, https://inside.fifa.com/tournament-organisation/partners

135 FIFA, "Aramco and FIFA Announce Global Partnership," April 25, 2024, https://inside.fifa.com/tournament-organisation/commercial/media-releases/aramco-and-fifa-announce-global-partnership

136 Tariq Saleh, "FIFA Adds Marriott Bonvoy as Regional World Cup Partner," *Sportcal*, January 7, 2026, https://www.sportcal.com/news/fifa-adds-marriott-bonvoy-as-regional-world-cup-partner/?cf-view

137 Henry Bushnell, "FIFA to Allow Cut-Away TV Commercials During 2026 World Cup 'Hydration Breaks'," *New York Times*, March 5, 2026, https://www.nytimes.com/athletic/7081341/2026/03/05/world-cup-hydration-breaks-tv-commercials-ads/

138 FIFA, "FIFA Council Approves Record-Breaking FIFA World Cup 2026™ Financial Contribution," December 17, 2025, https://inside.fifa.com/organisation/fifa-council/media-releases/council-approves-record-breaking-world-cup-2026-financial-contribution

139 Henry Bushnell, "FIFA to Use Dynamic Pricing for World Cup Tickets," *New York Times*, September 3, 2025, https://www.nytimes.com/athletic/6593901/2025/09/03/world-cup-2026-tickets-fifa-dynamic-pricing/

140 Trevor Noah, "Is the World Cup Rigged?" February 2025, https://www.youtube.com/watch?v=uhgOaUPs9LY

141 Dave Zirin and Jules Boykoff, "Zohran Mamdani Is Right to Call Out FIFA. But He Doesn't Go Far Enough." *The Nation,* October 10, 2025, https://www.thenation.com/article/society/zohran-mamdani-fifa-ice/

142 FIFA, "Tournament Access for Low-Income Groups," nd, https://publications.fifa.com/fr/final-sustainability-report/social-pillar/inclusivity/tournament-access-for-low-income-groups/

143 FIFA, "New Ticket Pricing Tier Introduced for Fans of Qualified Teams at FIFA World Cup 2026™," December 16, 2025, https://www.fifa.com/en/tournaments/mens/worldcup/canadamexicousa2026/articles/fifa-world-cup-2026-new-ticket-pricing-tier

144 Jules Boykoff, "Zohran Mamdani Has Upended US Politics. Now He Should Take on FIFA," *Guardian,* November 8, 2025, https://www.theguardian.com/football/2025/nov/08/zohran-mamdani-has-upended-us-politics-now-he-should-take-on-fifa; Cai, "US Cities Confront FIFA Over World Cup Costs."

145 Alexander Abnos, "Trump Threatens Removal of World Cup Games from Boston, Olympics from LA," *Guardian,* October 14, 2025, https://www.theguardian.com/sport/2025/oct/14/trump-world-cup-olympics-threat-boston Technically Foxborough, Massachusetts—located 22 miles southwest of Boston—is hosting matches, not Boston.

146 Adam Crafton, "FIFA Fan Fest for New York/New Jersey Cancelled Four Months Before World Cup," *New York Times,* February 20, 2026, https://www.nytimes.com/

athletic/7060549/2026/02/20/world-cup-2026-fifa-fan-new-york-new-jersey-cancelled/

147 Henry Bushnell, "World Cup Parking for $300? FIFA Selling Spots at L.A. Games for More than Tickets," *New York Times*, February 2, 2026, https://www.nytimes.com/athletic/7010484/2026/02/02/2026-fifa-world-cup-parking-prices/

148 Dave Zirin, "Trump and His Soulless Cronies Have Managed to Suck the Joy Out of the World Cup," *The Nation*, March 5, 2026, https://www.thenation.com/article/world/world-cup-trump-infantino-ice/

149 Boykoff, "Zohran Mamdani Has Upended US Politics"; Personal interview with Bob Mackin, November 4, 2025.

150 Talia Richie, "Homeless Advocates Concerned GTA Respite Centre Is Closing Early for World Cup Despite Tough Winter," *CBC*, February 11, 2025, https://www.cbc.ca/news/canada/toronto/especially-cold-winter-homeless-response-9.7084618

151 Diego Valverde, "Mexico to Deploy Counter-Drone Systems for 2026 World Cup," *Mexico Business News*, March 3, 2026, https://mexicobusiness.news/tech/news/mexico-deploy-counter-drone-systems-2026-world-cup; James Wagner and David Shortell, "Here Is Mexico's Plan to Keep the Country Safe During the World Cup," *New York Times*, March 6, 2026, https://www.nytimes.com/2026/03/06/world/americas/world-cup-mexico-security-plan.html

152 Homeland Security Republicans, "Chairman Garbarino Announces Hearing on Federal, State, Local Coordination for FIFA World Cup, America 250," February 19, 2026, https://

homeland.house.gov/2026/02/19/media-advisory-chairman-garbarino-announces-hearing-on-federal-state-local-coordination-for-fifa-world-cup-america-250/

153 Jules Boykoff and Dave Zirin, "Trump's World Cup Will Endanger Foreign Guests. Boycott Now!" *The Nation*, May 20, 2025, https://www.thenation.com/article/society/trump-world-cup-boycott/

154 Colin Millar, "ICE Says It Will Play 'Key Part' in 2026 World Cup Security," *New York Times*, February 11, 2026, https://www.nytimes.com/athletic/7038337/2026/02/11/world-cup-usa-ice-security/

155 US Department of State, "Welcoming the World: US PreparationsfortheFIFAWorldCup26™"December3,2025, https://www.state.gov/briefings-foreign-press-centers/preparations-for-fifa-world-cup-2026

156 Boykoff and Zirin, "Trump's World Cup Will Endanger Foreign Guests."

157 Radley Balko, "Trump's Immigration Nightmare: It *Is* Happening Here," *The New Republic*, December 24, 2025, https://newrepublic.com/article/204227/trump-immigration-nightmare-happening-here

158 "German Soccer Club Cancels US Trip Amid Concerns Over ICE Actions in Minnesota." *Reuters*, February 20, 2026, https://www.theguardian.com/football/2026/feb/20/werder-bremen-cancel-us-trip-minnesota-ice

159 Berries Bossmann, " 'FIFA Is a Dictatorship': A Former FIFA President Lashes Out at His Successor's Trump Ties," *Politico*, February 27, 2026, https://www.politico.com/news/2026/02/27/fifa-is-a-dictatorship-a-former-

fifa-president-lashes-out-at-his-successors-trump-ties-00802745

160 Federal Register, "Agency Information Collection Activities; Revision; Arrival and Departure Record (Form I-94) and Electronic System for Travel Authorization (ESTA). A Notice by the U.S Customs and Border Protection," December 10, 2025, https://www.federalregister.gov/d/2025-22461

161 Barney Ronay, "Infantino's Idolization of Trump Has Left Football With Blood on Its Hands," *Guardian*, March 2, 2026, https://www.theguardian.com/football/2026/mar/02/fifa-gianni-infantino-idolisation-donald-trump-football-world-cup-us-israel-middle-east

162 Bossmann, "'FIFA Is A Dictatorship'."

163 "Sepp Blatter Says On-Pitch Racism Can Be Resolved with Handshake," *BBC*, November 16, 2011, https://www.bbc.com/sport/football/15757165

164 Tom Hennigan, "FIFA President Strikes a Discordant Note at World Cup Draw," December 7, 2013, https://www.irishtimes.com/sport/soccer/international/fifa-president-strikes-a-discordant-note-at-world-cup-draw-1.1619989

165 Marcus Christenson and Paul Kelso, "Soccer Chief's Plan to Boost Women's Game? Hotpants," *Guardian*, January 16, 2004, https://www.theguardian.com/uk/2004/jan/16/football.gender

166 Jonathan Harding, "Lise Klaveness: 'Football Is in a Critical Time'," *DW*, April 2, 2025, https://www.dw.com/en/lise-klaveness-football-is-in-a-critical-time/a-72113399

167 Samindra Kunti, "Klaveness Re-elected to Norwegian FA Chair," *Inside World Football*, March 2, 2026, https://

www.insideworldfootball.com/2026/03/02/klaveness-re-elected-norwegian-fa-chair-rules-peace-prize-protest-fifa-congress/

168 Giovanni Arrighi, *The Long Twentieth Century* (London and New York: Verso, 2010), 379.

169 Stanis Elsborg and Karim Zidan, "Saudi Arabia's Grip on World Sports," *Play the Game*, December 2024, 1-46.

170 Boykoff, "Toward a Theory of Sportswashing," 348; Adam Ettinger, "Saudi Arabia, Sports Diplomacy and Authoritarian Capitalism in World Politics," *International Journal of Sport Policy and Politics*, Vol. 15, Number 3 (2023): 531-547.

171 FIFA, "Saudi Fund for Development and FIFA Join Forces to Provide Financial Support for Sports Infrastructure in Developing Nations," November 24, 2025, https://inside.fifa.com/organisation/media-releases/saudi-fund-for-development-financial-support-sports-infrastructure-developing-nations

172 Ashleigh Fields, "9/11 Victim's Son on Trump-Saudi Crown Prince Meeting: 'Disgusting Display'," *The Hill*, November 20, 2025, https://thehill.com/homenews/administration/5614634-son-911-victim-denounces-trump/

173 "Trump Welcomes Saudi Crown Prince and Dismisses Intel Linking Him to Khashoggi Killing," *PBS News*, November 18, 2025, https://www.pbs.org/newshour/show/trump-welcomes-saudi-crown-prince-and-dismisses-intel-linking-him-to-khashoggi-killing

174 Editorial Board, "Who Attended Trump's Dinner for the Saudi Crown Prince?" *New York Times*, November 18, 2025,

https://www.nytimes.com/2025/11/18/us/politics/trump-saudi-dinner-guests.html; Roland Li, "Elon Musk, Marc Benioff, and Jensen Huang Join Trump's Saudi Dinner and Leave Away with AI Deals," *San Francisco Chronicle,* November 19, 2025, https://finance.yahoo.com/news/elon-musk-marc-benioff-jensen-200643531.html

175 "President Trump Meets with the White House Task Force on FIFA World Cup 2026," *ABC News,* November 17, 2025, https://www.youtube.com/watch?v=btTyTu-aWnc

176 Henry Bushnell, "Ronaldo, Trump, and MBS at the White House? This Is the World in 2025 (and the World Cup in 2026)," *New York Times,* November 19, 2025, https://www.nytimes.com/athletic/6819393/2025/11/19/ronaldo-trump-mbs-white-house/

177 "Explained: The Allegations Against Cristiano Ronaldo, the Case's Dismissal and What's Next," *New York Times,* February 21, 2023, https://www.nytimes.com/athletic/2800154/2021/06/30/explained-allegations-cristiano-ronaldo/

178 Donald Trump, Truth Social, November 20, 2025, https://truthsocial.com/@realDonaldTrump/posts/115580448819564585

179 Nick Miller, "Cristiano Ronaldo's Reduced Ban Is No Surprise—A World Cup Without Him Simply Won't Do," *New York Times,* November 25, 2025, https://www.nytimes.com/athletic/6837146/2025/11/25/cristiano-ronaldo-world-cup-red-card/

180 "Trump Hosts Messi, Inter Miami FC Team at the White House," *Fox 5 New York,* March 6, 2026, https://www.youtube.com/watch?v=M9GXKY3oR8U

181 Pablo Iglesias Maurer, "Messi and Inter Miami Were Wallpaper for Trump's Whims in Their White House Visit," *Guardian,* March 6, 2026, https://www.theguardian.com/football/2026/mar/05/inter-miami-messi-trump-white-house

182 "Trump Asks Juventus Squad for Views on Transgender Players During Awkward White House Visit," *Guardian,* June 19, 2025, https://www.theguardian.com/football/2025/jun/18/donald-trump-juventus-transgender-players-club-world-cup; Adam Crafton, "Weah, McKennie and Juventus' Surreal Audience with Trump—'A Bit Weird,'" *New York Times,* June 19, 2025, https://www.nytimes.com/athletic/6436693/2025/06/19/weah-juventus-trump-iran-war/

183 Holly Ellyatt, "From $1 Trillion Spending to F-35s, US-Saudi Pledges Aren't Done Deals Yet," *CNBC,* November 19, 2025, https://www.cnbc.com/2025/11/19/from-1-trillion-spending-to-f-35s-us-saudi-pledges-arent-done-deals-yet.html

184 Lauren Hirsch, "Saudi Arabia, Once Shunned, Has Corporate Titans Swooning for Deals," *New York Times,* November 19, 2025, https://www.nytimes.com/2025/11/19/business/saudi-investment-forum-kennedy-center.html

185 Roll Call, "Donald Trump Addresses the US-Saudi Investment Forum in Washington," November 19, 2025, https://rollcall.com/factbase/trump/transcript/donald-trump-speech-us-saudi-investment-forum-november-19-2025/

186 Senate Democrats, "Transcript: President Trump Holds Bilat with Mohammed bin Salman of Saudi Arabia," November 18, 2025, https://www.democrats.senate.gov/newsroom/trump-transcripts/transcript-president-trump-holds-a-bilat-with-mohammed-bin-salman-of-saudi-arabia-111825

187 Stacy Perman, August Brown, and Samantha Masunaga, "Once a Pariah, Saudi Arabia Now Hollywood's Cash Source." *Los Angeles Times*, December 18, 2025, https://www.latimes.com/entertainment-arts/business/story/2025-12-18/hollywoods-hot-cash-source-previously-shunned-saudi-arabia

188 Michael Kranish, "After Helping Prince's Rise, Trump and Kushner Benefit from Saudi Funds," *Washington Post*, February 11, 2023, https://www.washingtonpost.com/politics/2023/02/12/after-helping-princes-rise-trump-kushner-benefit-saudi-funds/

189 Vivian Nereim and Rebecca R. Ruiz, "Trump Organization Is Said to Be in Talks on a Saudi Government Real Estate Deal," *New York Times*, November 15, 2025, https://www.nytimes.com/2025/11/15/world/middleeast/trump-organization-saudi-development-deal.html

190 Lauren Aratani, "Trump Accused of 'Corruption, Plain and Simple' After UAE Invested in Family Firm," *Guardian*, February 2, 2026, https://www.theguardian.com/us-news/2026/feb/02/trump-uae-crypto-deal

191 David Uberti, Juanje Gómez, and Karen Dapena, "The Trump Family Business Empire Is Growing. We Mapped Out 268 Pieces of It," *Wall Street Journal*, December 18, 2025,

https://www.wsj.com/politics/trump-family-business-visualized-6d132c71

192 Jules Boykoff and Dave Zirin, "With ICE Out of Control, How Can the US Cohost the 2026 World Cup?" *The Nation*, March 31, 2025, https://www.thenation.com/article/world/ice-fifa-world-cup-north-america/

193 Ivan Pech and Sean Jacobs, "Boycott Talk," *Eleven Named People*, February 5, 2026, https://elevennamedpeople.substack.com/p/boycott-talk

194 Paul Darby, "Politics, Resistance, and Patronage: The African Boycott of the 1966 World Cup and Its Ramifications," *Soccer & Society*, Vol. 20, Numbers 7-8 (2019): 936-947.

195 Chris Lee, *The Defiant: A History of Football Against Fascism* (Chichester: Pitch Publishing, 2022).

196 Karim Zidan, "The Empty Threat of a World Cup Boycott," *Sports Politika*, January 28, 2026, https://www.sportspolitika.news/p/world-cup-boycott-trump-europe-sports-politics; Dave Zirin, "A Call Is Rising for Nations to Boycott the Trump World Cup," *The Nation*, January 27, 2026, https://www.thenation.com/article/society/oke-goettlich-world-cup-boycott/; UK Parliament, "International Sport and Alleged United States Violations of International Law," January 6, 2026, https://edm.parliament.uk/early-day-motion/65002

197 Eco, "Sports Chatter," 159, 160.

198 Personal interview with Eric Sheehan, March 6, 2026.

199 Personal interview with Ajamu Baraka, March 9, 2026.

200 Stevphen Shukaitis, "The Trequartistas of Culture," *e-flux Journal*, Issue 158, November 2025, https://www.e-flux.com/journal/158/6776801/the-trequartistas-of-culture

201 Olúfẹ́mi O. Táíwò, *Elite Capture: How the Powerful Took Over Identity Politics (And Everything Else)* (Chicago: Haymarket Books, 2022), 22.

202 Kyle Fruh, Alfred Archer, Jake Wojtowicz, *The Ethics of Sportswashing* (London and New York: Routledge, 2026).

203 FIFA, "FIFA Statutes," May 2024, 12.

204 FIFA, "Strategic Objectives for the Global Game: 2023-2027," n.d., https://inside.fifa.com/strategic-objectives-2023-2027

205 Callum McCloskey, David McGillivray, Gayle McPherson, and Adam Talbot, "Institutionalizing Human Rights in Sports Mega Events: A Case Study of the United 2026 FIFA Men's World Cup," *Soccer & Society* (March 11, 2026): 1-20.

206 FIFA, "FIFA Statutes," May 2024, 12.

207 FIFA, "Code of Ethics," 2023, 16.

208 FIFA, "FIFA Statutes," May 2024, 57.

209 Jules Boykoff, "FIFA Banned Russia from International Football. Now It Must Do the Same for Israel," *Guardian*, September 25, 2025, https://www.theguardian.com/football/2025/sep/25/fifa-banned-russia-from-international-football-now-it-must-do-the-same-for-israel

210 Jules Boykoff and Dave Zirin, "2 FIFA Rulings on Israel, 1 Familiar Deference to MAGA," *The Nation*, March 24, 2026, https://www.thenation.com/article/society/fifa-israel-rulings-complicity-world-cup/

211 Boykoff and Zirin, "Trump's World Cup Will Endanger Foreign Guests."

212 FIFA, "FIFA and the Board of Peace Announce Strategic Partnership to Drive Recovery and Peace Through

Football," February 19, 2026, https://inside.fifa.com/organisation/media-releases/board-of-peace-strategic-partnership-recovery-peace-gaza?requester=MediaHub

213 Zvika Klein, "Who Is Yakir Gabay, the Billionaire on Trump's Gaza Board of Peace?" *Jerusalem Post*, January 22, 2026, https://www.jpost.com/opinion/article-884287

214 FairSquare, "Substitute," 7.

215 FairSquare, "Substitute," 169.

216 Natalie Koch, "Athletic Autocrats: Understanding Images of Authoritarian Leaders as Sportsmen," in Natalie Koch (ed.) *Critical Geographies of Sport: Space, Power and Sport in Global Perspective* (New York: Routledge, 2017), 91-107.

217 S.V. Date, "Second-Term Tab for Trump's Golf Hobby Tops $70 Million, On Track to Exceed $300 Million," *Huffington Post*, November 26, 2025, https://www.huffpost.com/entry/trump-golf-300-million_n_69271f3ce4b00aca68d3d689

218 Karim Zidan, "Donald Trump's UFC Stunt is More Than a Circus. It's Authoritarian Theatre," *Guardian*, July 5, 2025, https://www.theguardian.com/sport/2025/jul/05/trump-ufc-white-house-authoritarian-spectacle

219 Donald Trump, Truth Social, March 5, 2026, https://truthsocial.com/@realDonaldTrump/posts/116178030946996760

220 Priyanash, "With Friends Like These," *Eleven Named People*, January 22, 2026, https://elevennamedpeople.substack.com/p/with-friends-like-these

221 René Hauri and Philipp Rindlisbacher, "In Diktaturen Ist Es Für Uns Einfacher" *Tages Anzeiger*, April 2, 2019, https://www.tagesanzeiger.ch/sport/ski-wm/in-diktaturen-ist-es-fuer-uns-einfacher/story/26126306

222 Dakota Smith, "After Epstein Files, Wasserman's Survival as LA Olympics Chief May Come Down to Money," *Los Angeles Times*, February 24, 2026, https://www.latimes.com/california/story/2026-02-24/after-epstein-files-wassermans-survival-as-la-olympics-chief-may-come-down-to-money

223 Personal interview with Victor Quintero, March 9, 2026.

Acknowledgments

Big thanks to everyone at OR Books who helped make *Red Card* a reality: Sam Russek, Colin Robinson, Olivia Heffernan, Bella Isaacson, Georgie Carr, Ana Ratner, Antara Ghosh, and Fatema Merchant. Thanks be to Susan Schoenbeck, Eunjin Park, and Molly Boykoff for research assistance. And thank you to the extraordinary library staff at Pacific University who step up time and again: Jennifer Bosvert, Michelle Lenox, Justyne Triest, Jerica Tullo, and Kyle Webb. Thanks also to Dean Jaye Cee Whitehead of Pacific University for financial support. Finally, thanks go to Dave Zirin—friend, editor, co-author, comrade.

Author Photograph © Kaia Sand

Jules Boykoff is the author of *Kicking,* a memoir about his former life as a professional soccer player and his current life as a critical academic of sport. He has written six books on the politics of the Olympic Games, including *What Are the Olympics For?, NOlympians: Inside the Fight Against Capitalist Mega-Sports in Los Angeles, Tokyo, and Beyond,* and *Power Games: A Political History of the Olympics.* His work has appeared in outlets such as *The Nation, The Guardian, The Los Angeles Times, The New York Times, The Globe and Mail, Jacobin, Folha de São Paulo,* and *Common Dreams.* Boykoff teaches political science at Pacific University.

www.ingramcontent.com/pod-product-compliance
Lightning Source LLC
Jackson TN
JSHW021901250426
101322JS00001B/1

* 9 7 8 1 6 8 2 1 9 5 2 8 4 *